Advising Mentally Disordered Offenders

ADVISING MENTALLY DISORDERED OFFENDERS

A Practical Guide

DEBORAH POSTGATE
and
CAROLYN TAYLOR

law society publishing

ISBN 1 85328 685 0

Published in 2000 by the Law Society
113 Chancery Lane, London WC2A 1PL

Typeset by J&L Composition Ltd, Filey, North Yorkshire
Printed by Antony Rowe Ltd, Chippenham, Wilts

Contents

APPENDICES

Preface

In the past few years, there have been a number of inquiries into deaths caused by the actions of mentally disordered people. A small number of patients who have been discharged into the community or failed to be admitted to hospital, have committed these acts of violence which have become a source of national concern.

During the course of the inquiries, the role of the legal representative both at the police station and in the magistrates' court has frequently been examined and in some cases, criticised. Partly as a response to these criticisms, which focus on lack of training of lawyers in dealing with mentally disordered offenders, the Law Society has commissioned this book. The Legal Aid Board duty solicitor committee will require all duty solicitors to have access to a copy of the book.

We have assumed that the reader has a basic knowledge of giving advice in the police station and access to the following: *Advising a Suspect in the Police Station* by Anthony Edwards (Sweet & Maxwell, 1997); *Police Station Skills for Legal Advisers* by Eric Shepherd, a training kit with four books including *A Pocket Reference* (also sold separately), an Activity Log and two cassettes (The Law Society, 1996); and *Defending Suspects at the Police Station* by Ed Cape with Jawaid Luqmani (Legal Action Group, 1999). The text of this book covers law and procedures in the police station and magistrates' courts only; it does not deal with contested trials in the magistrates' courts or crown court procedures.

The book is written from our shared experience and consultation with other professionals such as psychiatrists and social workers. It is not an academic work but rather a practical guide to advising mentally disordered offenders. We do not profess to be experts in the medical field of mental health and thus Chapter 1 should be read as a guide to identifying signs and symptoms of mental disorder. Particular thanks are due to Dr James MacKeith, consultant forensic psychiatrist, for contributing to and correcting this chapter.

As a consequence of the Human Rights Act 1999 and the review of the Mental Health Act 1983 together with the Government's current proposals for the detention of dangerous people with severe personality disorder, there are likely to be changes in the law relating to the rights of people with mental health problems. It is beyond the scope of this book to comment on these developments.

We would like to express our thanks to all those who read and commented on various parts of the text.

The law is as stated at 1 January 2000.

Deborah Postgate
Carolyn Taylor

Table of cases

Table of statutes

Table of secondary legislation

CHAPTER 1

Mental disorder: medical and legal definitions

1.1 Terminology

1.1.1 Section 1 (2)(a) of the Mental Health Act 1983 (The Act) defines 'mental disorder' as:

> '... *mental illness, arrested or incomplete development of mind, psychopathic disorder or any other disorder or disability of mind*'.

The term mental disorder is generic and is used throughout the Police and Criminal Evidence Act 1984 (PACE) and its Codes of Practice.

1.1.2 This definition is a legal classification and should not be confused with medical and diagnostic terminology which is found in medical reports and records. The medical diagnoses are described in the two recognised manuals for the classification of psychiatric diagnosis, the *International Classification of Diseases* 10th Edition (ICD 10) and the *Diagnostic and Statistical Manual of Disorders* Edition IV (DSM IV). The legal and medical methods of describing disorders do not necessarily harmonise; for instance, mental illness is a specific classification under the Act, but is not found in the manuals, whereas schizophrenia is not referred to in the Act but has a recognised medical diagnosis (ICD 10 F.20).

1.1.3 The Act stipulates that a person may not be treated as suffering from mental disorder by reason *only* of promiscuity or other immoral conduct, sexual deviancy or dependence on alcohol or drugs (s.1 (3)). However, a person may suffer from a mental disorder *as well as* one of the disorders listed in s.1 (3). In this case it is established in case law that compulsory treatment may be offered which deals with both disorders which are often inextricably linked. For example, a learning-disabled person with

1

seriously irresponsible behavioural problems, and thus detainable under the Act as mentally impaired, may also commit sexual offences with minors. Compulsory treatment is likely to be aimed at reducing his sexually deviant behaviour as well as his other difficulties. Persons who suffer psychosis as a consequence of the abuse of drink or drugs may be compulsorily treated as suffering from mental illness.

1.2 Mental illness

1.2.1 This term is not further defined in the Act but in its consultative document on the Mental Health Act 1959, the Department of Social Security defined this category as any disorder having one or more of the following characteristics:

(a) more than temporary impairment of intellectual functions shown by a failure of memory, orientation, comprehension and learning capacity;

(b) more than temporary alteration of mood of such degree as to give rise to the patient having a delusional appraisal of his situation, his past or future, or that of others or to the lack of any appraisal;

(c) delusional beliefs persecutory, jealous or grandiose;

(d) abnormal perceptions associated with delusional misinterpretation of events;

(e) thinking so disordered as to prevent the patient making a reasonable appraisal of his situation or having reasonable communication with others.

1.2.2 It is generally agreed that the term mental illness covers disorders which have not always existed in the patient but have developed in him to become a condition which overlays the patient's personality when well (his 'pre-morbid' personality). Contrast, for example, 'arrested or incomplete development of mind' which may well date from birth.

1.2.3 There are many psychiatric diagnoses which exhibit some of the characteristics listed at para. 1.2.1. ICD 10 categorises the disorders most likely to fall into the legal category of mental illness:

(a) **organic mental disorder**, e.g. dementia, behavioural disorder due to brain disease or injury;

(b) **mental and behavioural disorder** due to substance abuse, e.g. alcohol or drug dependency resulting in psychotic disorders or withdrawal state;

(c) **neurotic, stress-related disorders**, often with an external cause, e.g. anxiety, post-traumatic stress disorder, obsessive–compulsive disorder;

(d) **behavioural syndromes** associated with physical factors, e.g. sleeping and eating disorders (including anorexia nervosa, which has been recognised as a mental illness for the purposes of the Act);

(e) **personality disorders**, e.g. narcissistic personality disorders (see also psychopathic disorder at para. 1.4);

(f) **schizophrenia**, which also comes under the mental illness category. It is a generic term for a group of diseases which have certain signs and symptoms in common but may not have either the same presentation or similar prognoses. Schizophrenia occurs in several clinical forms; simple, hebephrenic, catatonic, paranoid and residual. If there is a large affective (mood) component the expression 'schizo-affective disorder' may be used. Schizotypal and delusional disorders are often encountered.

1.2.4 Paranoid schizophrenia is characterised by the person believing he is in a hostile environment either as a result of a misinterpretation of the actions of others or as the result of a complex delusional system which may dominate his thinking and reactions. People with paranoid illnesses often get into trouble with the police and you are therefore more likely to come across this form of schizophrenia. Many of the characteristics noted in the defining features of mental illness in para. 1.2.1 may also be present, but the more typical symptoms include:

(a) delusions – false beliefs which cannot be altered in the face of incontrovertible evidence or reasoned argument, for example, believing that alien beings have you under observation and intend you harm;

(b) auditory hallucinations – false perceptions that are most commonly seen in the form of voices or visions perceived by the person, in the absence of any obvious source or without any basis in external reality;

(c) incoherence of speech, flat or grossly inappropriate responses.

1.2.5 If your client suffers from schizophrenia he may become socially withdrawn, be regarded as eccentric, is more likely to be a victim of assault provoked by his own erratic behaviour, and be at risk of self-destructive and suicidal behaviour (one in ten people who have schizophrenia die from suicide). He may also display anti-social and violent behaviour.

1.2.6 Many clients may resist or refute the diagnosis of their condition. It is rare for a client to state openly that he suffers from schizo-phrenia, especially when detained in the police station. It may be possible to make an educated guess about your client's clinical diagnosis by establishing what medication has been prescribed for him. Common medications for the treatment of schizophrenic illness include:

Drug	Trade Name	
Chlorpromazine	Largactil	
Trifluperazine	Stelazine	
Droperidol	Droleptan	
Risperidone	Risperdal	oral
Sulpiride	Sulparex	
	Sulpitil	
	Dolmatil	
*Clozapine	Clozaril	
Flupenthixol	Depixol	
Fluphenazine	Modecate	
Zuclopenthixol	Clopixol	depot injection
Haloperidol	Haldol	

*Treatment with Clozaril requires regular blood tests. A patient receiving this medication is likely to have a good history of compliance with treatment.

4

1.2.7 **Mood (affective) disorders**, e.g. manic episodes, bipolar affective disorder (where the patient has a period of 'high' mood followed swiftly by a depressed phase). Manic symptoms include elevated, expansive or irritable moods, characterised by over-activity and restlessness, grandiose beliefs, flight of ideas, racing thoughts and speech.

Physical treatment for affective disorders includes:

(a) Lithium carbonate (trade name Priadel);

(b) Lithium citrate;

(c) Carbamazepine (trade name Tegretol);

(d) Sodium valporate;

(e) Electro convulsive therapy (ECT).

1.2.8 Depressive episode: typical symptoms include lethargy, persistent depressed mood, loss of weight, disturbed sleep patterns, morbid and guilty thoughts including thoughts of self-harm and suicide. Severe depression may be associated with psychotic symptoms.

Treatment for depression includes:

(a) Ampitryptiline (trade name Tryptizol);

(b) Clomipramine (trade name Anafranil);

(c) Trimipramine (trade name Surmontil);

(d) Fluoxetine (trade name Prozac);

(e) ECT which is used in highly selective cases of very severe depression.

1.3 Arrested or incomplete development of mind

1.3.1 This term is broken down later in the Act to include two levels of disorder, *mental impairment* and *severe mental impairment*. Both of these conditions are mental disorders for the purposes of the Act and differ from each other only in degree. Mental impairment is defined in the Act as:

*'a state of arrested or incomplete development of mind which
includes significant impairment of intelligence or social functioning and is associated with abnormally aggressive or seriously
irresponsible conduct'.*

The definition of severe mental impairment is identical save that
the word 'significant' is replaced by 'severe'. However, note that in
both cases there must be abnormally aggressive or seriously irresponsible conduct to trigger the working of the Act. In addition, a
mentally impaired person can only be detained for treatment
under s.3 of the Act if he is considered treatable.

1.3.2 The clinical term 'learning disability' is usually used to describe
people in this category of mental disorder although the PACE
Codes of Practice use the term mental handicap. Other terms
which are sometimes used include learning difficulties, develop-
mental disability and intellectual disability. Learning disability
covers various conditions and manifestations. In some people,
learning disability is the direct result of organic damage, such as
malfunction of the nervous system during or shortly after birth.
Others have a chromosomal abnormality such as Down's
syndrome or have no known organic defects. Learning disability is
sometimes qualified with the terms, 'mild', 'moderate', 'severe' or
'profound' according to the severity of the disability.

1.3.3 Assessment of learning disabilities combines assessment of intellectual, behavioural and social skills. People who have intellectual
or cognitive deficit are measured by performance in IQ tests.
Mental impairment generally covers those falling in the IQ range
50–70, while below 50 is taken to be severe impairment. However,
note the Court of Appeal decision in the case of *R* v. *Silcott,
Braithwaite and Raghip* (1991) The Times, 9 December where it
was accepted that an IQ of 75 amounted to a mental handicap and
this contributed to the exclusion of confession evidence. Stress was
laid on the need to assess each individual's abilities, rather than the
exact IQ figure. A guidance booklet, *Competent to Tell the Truth*
produced by Voice UK, sets out very helpful advice on identifying
people with learning disabilities and ways of assessing their
competence as witnesses.

1.4   Psychopathic disorder

1.4.1 This term is defined by the Act as:

> '*a persistent disorder or disability of mind (whether or not including significant impairment of intelligence) which results in abnormally aggressive or seriously irresponsible conduct*'.

1.4.2 To result in a treatment order under the Act, the condition must be considered 'treatable', i.e. that hospital treatment is likely to alleviate or prevent a deterioration in the condition. 'Treatment' has a wide definition, however, and can include nursing care or supervision within a structured setting, i.e. a secure hospital (see the House of Lords case *Hutchison Reid* v. *Secretary of State for Scotland* 1999 SLT 279). It is a matter of longstanding debate whether a psychopathic disorder is treatable and whether offenders so diagnosed should go through the hospital or the penal system. In practice, it is often the seriousness of the risk posed by the psychopathic offender which will determine whether or not lengthy and costly treatment is considered worthwhile.

1.4.3 The legal term 'psychopathic disorder' will often embrace more than one specific diagnosed form of personality disorders in the ICD 10 and DSM IV diagnostic manuals. Of those labelled with the legal term 'psychopathic disorder' many are likely to be people attracting the medical diagnostic term 'psychopathic disorder' and 'dissocial personality'. See ICD 10 F.60 which describes a wide range of diagnosed personality disorders, including dissocial personality disorder (F.60.2), paranoid personality (F.60.0), emotionally unstable personality disorder (F.60.30, F.60.31) and borderline personality disorder (F.60.31). The disorder of dissocial personality must be longstanding and is inferred from evidence of persistent antisocial or culturally deviant behaviour, characterised by a lack of social responsibility, consideration for others, judgement and foresight. It can often result in irresponsible and aggressive behaviour. Personality disorders are apparent by late childhood or adolescence otherwise the diagnosis cannot be made. They are not secondary to any organic cause or any other mental disorder although they can coexist with other disorders.

1.5 Any other disorder or disability of mind

1.5.1 This term is not defined further in the Act and seems to be applied to any mental disorder not falling within one of the definitions above. A person can be detained in hospital under s.2 of the Act for assessment for a maximum of 28 days under this category of mental disorder. He cannot be made subject to a treatment order under s.3 of the Act because to do so he must suffer from a disorder falling within one of the first three categories in s.1 (2) of the Act, that is, mental illness, arrested or incomplete development of mind or psychopathic disorder.

CHAPTER 2
Procedures in the police station

2.1 The sources of mental health law

2.1.1 A list of the relevant legislation, codes of practice and guidances, which are referred to throughout the text and with which representatives should familiarise themselves when working in this area of law, is set out in Appendix 1. Of these, the most important are the Mental Health Act 1983 and the Code of Practice pursuant to s.118 of the Act, Home Office circulars and guidances, and the Police and Criminal Evidence Act 1984 together with the Codes of Practice issued under s.66 of PACE. Code C, Annex E of these Codes of Practice summarises the provisions relating to mentally disordered and mentally handicapped people at the police station. Additional references are contained in Code C itself, and in two other sections of the Codes. The Home Office guidance/circulars contain useful statements on diverting the mentally disordered offender so that he receives appropriate treatment rather than be put through the criminal justice system.

2.2 Legal aid

2.2.1 As with any suspect at the police station, a mentally disordered person is entitled to free legal advice, which is not means tested. At the end of the police station stage of the case you will complete CLAIM14 and CLAIM15 (if you acted as duty solicitor) and, if there has been a hearing for a warrant for further detention, CLAIM16.

2.2.2 It is also advisable to get your client to sign a CLAIM10 as there may be work to be done either if he is bailed to return to the police station at a later date or between charge and first appearance at court. If your client is too ill to sign the CLAIM10, regulation 14 of the Legal Advice and Assistance Regulations 1989 allows a solicitor to accept an application for advice and assistance from among others, the patient's receiver, nearest relative or guardian (as defined in the Act). Alternatively, any other person may make the application provided that the Area Director of the Legal Aid Board (LAB) is satisfied that it is reasonable in the circumstances and has given prior authority for the advice and assistance to be given to such person on behalf of the patient. This could include a social worker or a key worker. Franchised firms no longer have to get prior authority and can exercise their devolved powers in this situation.

2.3 Reason for detention

2.3.1 There are three reasons why a mentally disordered person may find himself being detained at the police station. The first two are under ss.135 and 136 of the Act and the third is on arrest for a criminal offence. Sections 135 and 136 should only be used by police as a stop-gap before transfer to hospital.

2.3.2 Section 135 of the Mental Health Act 1983 states that a magistrate, on receiving an information laid by an approved social worker, may issue a warrant authorising a police constable to enter any private premises for the purpose of removing to a place of safety, a person believed to be suffering from mental disorder. Any police officer may execute the warrant as the meaning of constable is the office of constable and not the rank of constable: Police Act 1964 s.18 sched. 2. The person must either have been or is being ill-treated, neglected or kept otherwise than under proper control or is living alone and unable to care for himself. When executing the warrant, the officer must be accompanied by an approved social worker and a registered medical practitioner.

2.3.3 The removal to a place of safety is with a view to the making of an application in respect of the person under Part II of the Act or of other arrangements regarding his treatment or care. The maximum length of time a person can be detained under s.135 is 72 hours from arrival at the place of safety.

2.3.4 Under s.135 (2), a magistrate has the power to issue a warrant to enter and remove a person who is already liable be detained under the Act. Sections 15 and 16 of PACE, which mainly set out the specific practice and procedure to be followed on issuing and executing warrants, apply to warrants issued under this section.

2.3.5 Section 136 of the Mental Health Act 1983 provides that a police constable on finding a person in a public place, who appears to him to be suffering from mental disorder *and* to be in immediate need of care and control, may remove that person to a place of safety. No medical evidence is required to substantiate the diagnosis of mental disorder prior to the removal, as the officer need only have a reasonable belief that the person is mentally disordered and that it is necessary to remove him in the interests of that person or for the protection of others. This section, unlike section 135, specifically requires the person, once detained at the place of safety, to be examined by a registered medical practitioner and interviewed by an approved social worker and for any necessary arrangements to be made for his care or treatment.

2.3.6 Points to note in sections 135 and 136

(a) Detention under the Act has no age limit and therefore children and youths of any age can be removed and detained under ss.135 and 136.

(b) Section 135(6) includes a police station in its definition of a place of safety. When the Act came into force it was envisaged that if the place of safety had to be a police station then it should only be used in exceptional circumstances and for a few hours. Home Office Circular 66/90 (see Appendix 5) and the Mental Health Act Code of Practice, para. 10(5) advises that, wherever possible, the place of safety should be a hospital and not a police station. The police service should draw up suitable arrangements with local health authorities and social services departments for the detention and assessment of mentally disordered people. The Inter-Agency Working Document (issued with Home Office Circular 12/95) points out that police stations do not have the facilities necessary for the welfare of such people and detention in them is likely to be damaging to their health. You should be aware of the local arrangements in existence for a place of safety. Note also that a person cannot be removed from one place of safety to another.

(c) Even though a person detained under ss.135 and 136 is not under arrest, the PACE Codes of Practice apply to them (Code C, para. 1.10). Detainees under both ss.135 and 136

11

have a right to consult a solicitor in private and receive in-dependent free legal advice. In addition, s.26 and Schedule 2 to PACE preserve the power to arrest under s.136 and hence the person has all the rights under PACE of a person arrested on suspicion of a criminal offence. The Mental Health Act Code of Practice (para. 10.9) also confirms that although the Act uses the term 'remove', it is deemed to be an 'arrest' for the purposes of PACE. It follows, therefore, that a police constable who has detained a person under s.136 is empowered to search him.

(d) As the PACE Codes of Practice apply to a person detained under ss.135 and 136 the custody officer should also inform an appropriate adult of the person's detention and request that they attend the police station. Most custody officers are of the view that this obligation is fulfilled by calling the approved social worker to the police station to interview and examine the person. However, there may be a conflict between the detainee and the approved social worker, for example, if he wants the detainee sectioned and the detainee does not want to go into hospital. In this situation, an inde-pendent appropriate adult should be called. If your client is also detained in respect of a criminal matter then an appro-priate adult must be asked to attend the station. You should always check with the custody officer whether an appropriate adult has been called and ask that one be contacted if that has not been done.

(e) Under para. 3.10 of Code C there is an obligation on the police to ensure that a person detained under s.136 be assessed as soon as possible. If that assessment is to take place at the police station then an approved social worker and registered medical practitioner must be called to the police station as soon as possible to interview and examine the detainee. This requirement absolves the custody officer from his obligation to call a police surgeon under Code C para. 9.2. and Annex E para. 5. The custody officer has discretion not to call the surgeon so long as he believes that the assessment by a registered medical practitioner can be undertaken without undue delay. Once this has been done and arrangements have been made for the detainee's treatment or care, he can no longer be detained under s.136. The Mental Health Act Code of Practice (para. 10.18) states that where the police station has been used as a place of safety and the assessors are of the view that compulsory detention is indicated, then the person should be admitted to hospital under ss.2 or 3 of the Act. When it is more urgent, admission under s.4 of the Act must be considered.

(f) Paragraph 10.14(b) of the Mental Health Act Code of Practice confirms that if it appears that the person detained under s.136 has a learning disability, it is desirable for a consultant psychiatrist specialising in learning disabilities and an approved social worker with experience of working with people with learning disabilities to be available to make a joint assessment.

(g) Paragraph 10.8 of the same Code states that ordinarily the police should not discharge a person detained under s.136 before the end of the 72-hour period without the assessments having taken place within that period. Where a doctor, having examined the detainee, concludes that he is not mentally disordered within the meaning of the Act then he can no longer be detained under the section and should be immediately discharged from detention.

2.3.7 If you are instructed by a person detained under ss.135 or 136 you should, on first speaking to the client, try and establish if there is a history of contact with mental health services so that where possible, contact can be made with either a treating doctor or key worker to ensure that an assessment takes place as soon as possible. If the treating doctor is unable to attend the police station, ask him to make contact with the doctor who subsequently examines your client. Your role is to ensure as far as possible that, particularly in relation to s.136, the police powers of arrest have been reasonably and properly exercised and that your client is detained appropriately. You must also make sure that he is going to be examined as soon as possible (and in any event within 72 hours) with a view to either release or transfer to hospital.

Arrest on suspicion of committing a criminal offence

2.3.8 Once a person has been arrested on suspicion of a criminal offence the police should take him to the police station as soon as possible.

2.4 The role and duties of the custody officer in relation to mentally disordered suspects

2.4.1 If a custody officer has any suspicion or is told in good faith that a person of any age may be mentally disordered, mentally handicapped or mentally incapable of understanding the significance of questions put to him or his replies, then that person shall be treated as being a mentally disordered or mentally handicapped person for the purposes of the Codes of Practice (Code C, para. 1.4 and Annex E, para. 1). The Notes for Guidance para. 1G confirm that where the custody officer has any doubt about the mental state or capacity of a person detained, an appropriate adult should be called.

2.4.2 It is extremely important to establish as early as possible whether the detainee falls into one of the categories listed in para. 2.4.1. The custody officer can be informed by anyone which can include the detainee's legal representative. A relative, or the client himself, may tell you and if that is the case, your client's authority to disclose this information to the police must be sought.

2.4.3 Once the custody officer authorises the detention of a person falling under Code C, para. 1.4 and Annex E, para. 1 he must, as soon as is practicable, ask an appropriate adult to attend the police station to see the person and inform the adult of the grounds for detention. (Code C, para. 3.9 and Annex E, para. 3). Action to inform the appropriate adult must still be taken even if your client is being detained on suspicion of having committed a serious arrestable offence and the provisions of Annex B to Code C, delaying the suspect's right to legal advice and the right to have someone informed of his arrest, apply.

2.4.4 In the case of *R.* v. *Aspinall* (1999) The Times, 4 February a suspect who suffered from schizophrenia, but was exhibiting no symptoms and had been examined by the police surgeon and deemed fit for detention and interview, still required the presence of an appropriate adult at the police station. The fact that the suspect was 'lucid in thought and oriented in time and space' did not negate the obligation on the custody officer to call an appropriate adult. The court held that the question which had to be determined was not whether the appellant's condition obviated the need for an appropriate adult to be present, but whether the admission of the evidence from the interview would have had such an adverse effect upon fairness that it should have been excluded.

2.4.5 Code C, para. 9.2 and Annex E, para. 5 set out the custody officer's obligation to call a police surgeon when a mentally disordered person is brought to the station. A similar obligation arises to a person *already detained* who subsequently appears to be mentally disordered. The relevant criteria bringing this obligation into being are that the detainee:

(a) appears to be suffering from a mental disorder; or

(b) fails to respond normally to questions or conversation (other than through drunkenness alone).

The second criterion listed above tends to cover people with learning difficulties. The case of *R.* v. *Aspinall* referred to at para. 2.4.4 confirms that the custody officer should *not* rely on the advice of the police surgeon as to the suspect's condition before deciding whether to call the appropriate adult. A decision by the police surgeon that a suspect is fit to be detained and interviewed does not relieve the custody officer of his duty to call the appropriate adult.

2.4.6 If the detainee has been prescribed any medication prior to his arrest, the custody officer must consult the police surgeon before allowing him to use it. Once authorised, the officer is then responsible for the safekeeping of any medication and for ensuring that the person is given the opportunity to take it. (Code C, para. 9.5)

15

2.5 Appropriate adult

2.5.1 Who can be an appropriate adult? In the case of a person who is mentally disordered or mentally handicapped, the appropriate adult is defined by Code C, para. 1.7 and Annex E, para. 2 as:

(a) a relative, guardian or other person responsible for his care or custody;

(b) someone who has experience of dealing with mentally disordered or mentally handicapped people but who is not a police officer or employed by the police (such as an approved social worker as defined by the Act or a specialist social worker); or

(c) failing either of the above, some other responsible adult aged 18 or over who is not a police officer or employed by the police.

2.5.2 Paragraph 1E of the Notes for Guidance to Code C and para. E1 of Annex E recommend that the appropriate adult is someone who has experience or training in the care of mentally disordered or handicapped people. However, the wishes of the detainee as to who their appropriate adult is, should, if practicable, be respected.

2.5.3 Paragraph 1C of the Notes for Guidance to Code C states that a person should not be an appropriate adult if:

(a) he is suspected of involvement in the offence in question;

(b) is a victim;

(c) is a witness;

(d) is involved in the investigation or

(e) has received admissions prior to attending to act as the appropriate adult.

A solicitor or lay visitor may also not act as the appropriate adult. (Code C, Notes for Guidance 1F).

2.5.4 The presence of an appropriate adult can be very important and you should satisfy yourself that the person appointed is indeed 'appropriate'. If the alleged offence took place in, for example, a mental health hostel then a worker from that hostel would be inappropriate.

2.5.5 The issue as to who should and who should not be appointed an appropriate adult has been discussed in the following cases:

(a) In *DPP* v. *Blake* [1989] WLR 432, the court upheld a defendant's right to choose who he wanted as his appropriate adult. This case dealt with the often practised policy of local authorities not to allow a social worker to act as appropriate adult unless it is impossible to contact a suitable person or that person has refused to attend. The court took the view that an estranged parent, who was willing to attend the police station, could not be said to be suitable if the parent was someone with whom the defendant had no empathy.

(b) In *R.* v. *O'Neill* (Birmingham Crown Court, 16 October 1990) the court had to consider whether the detainee's current probation officer could be considered by the police to act as an appropriate adult. The court held that a probation officer, particularly in relation to a mentally handicapped person, is a person in some authority over him and should not really be the appropriate adult save in exceptional circumstances. A further problem that arose was that it would be very difficult to prevent a jury from knowing the defendant had previous convictions if his current probation officer acted as appropriate adult. The defendant had in fact asked that his common-law wife act as his appropriate adult and the police had refused. The court held that the police had no power to veto this request.

(c) In *R.* v. *Morse & others* [1991] Crim LR 195, the defendant's father acted as his appropriate adult. He turned out to have an IQ between 60 and 70 and was virtually illiterate. There was doubt as to whether he was capable of appreciating the gravity of the situation in which his son found himself. The court held that since the purpose of an appropriate adult was to advise the defendant, if the appropriate adult was incapable of giving advice, he was not appropriate.

(d) In *R. v. Jefferson, Skerritt, Readman and Keogh* (1993) 99 Cr App R 13 it was held that an appropriate adult, as defined in Code C, para. 1.7 who gave encouragement to a juvenile to tell the truth, did not fail in his duty to advise him under Note 13C of Code C then in force, nor did it make him an inappropriate adult. There was no duty to protect him from what the court decided was fair and proper questioning.

(e) In *R. v. W and another* [1993] Crim LR 1994 130, the mother of a juvenile, appointed appropriate adult, was said to have a mental illness and be mentally handicapped. It was submitted on behalf of the defendant, at the appeal against conviction, that the mother was herself someone who would have required the protection of an appropriate adult had she found herself under arrest and in those circumstances the confession made in interview in her mother's presence should not have been admitted. The court held that at the trial, the judge based his decision to allow the interviews to be put before the jury, on his own findings about her capacity at the time of the interview. While she was psychotic at the time and suffering from some form of intellectual deficit, her paranoid delusions were confined to her neighbours. Her thought processes were rational in discussing her family and she was therefore capable of fulfilling the role of appropriate adult at the time of the interview.

2.6 The role and duties of the appropriate adult in relation to mentally disordered suspects

2.6.1 The custody officer must advise all suspects that the appropriate adult is there to assist and advise them and that they can consult with the appropriate adult in private at any time. (Code C, para. 3.12)

2.6.2 The appropriate adult must be present when the provisions of Code C, paras. 3.1 to 3.5 (i.e. the detainee's right to have someone informed of his arrest, to consult privately with his solicitor and to consult the Codes of Practice) are complied with. If the detainee has already been through these procedures, they must be repeated in the presence of the appropriate adult.

2.6.3 An appropriate adult can exercise the right to legal advice even if the detainee has declined it (Code C, para. 3.13 and Annex E, para. 4). It is possible for you to find that the police are telephoning you on behalf of the appropriate adult rather than the detainee. As very few appropriate adults are aware of this right it is important to draw their attention to it in your general dealings with people who regularly act as appropriate adults. It is particularly important when dealing with someone who may not have the mental capacity to understand the significance of having a solicitor to represent them at the police station. Notes for Guidance paras. 3G and E2 state that if the detainee has exercised his right to legal advice, the custody officer should contact the solicitor straight away and not delay until the appropriate adult arrives at the police station.

2.6.4 If the suspect's detention is to be reviewed by a review officer or a superintendent, the appropriate adult must, if available at the time, be given an opportunity to make representations to the officer about the need for continuing detention (see Code C, paras. 15.1 and 15.2 and Annex E, para. 10).

2.6.5 An intimate or strip search of a mentally disordered or mentally handicapped person may only take place in the presence of an appropriate adult of the same sex, unless the detainee specifically requests the presence of a particular adult of the opposite sex. A strip search may take place in the absence of an appropriate adult only in cases of urgency where there is a risk of serious harm to the detainee or to others. (See Code C, Annex A, paras. 5 and 11(c)).

2.6.6 Any procedure requiring the consent of a person who is mentally disordered or handicapped is only valid if given in the presence of an appropriate adult. This covers identification by witnesses, fingerprints and body samples and impressions as well as the taking of a photograph of the detainee by the police. (Code D, para. 1.11). Paragraph 1.14 emphasises that any procedure in Code D (Code of Practice for the Identification of Persons by Police Officers) involving the participation of a person, whether a suspect or a witness who is mentally disordered or handicapped, must take place in the presence of the appropriate adult; but the adult must not be allowed to prompt any identification of a suspect by a witness.

2.6.7 A mentally disordered or handicapped person must not be interviewed or asked to provide or sign a written statement (including comments recorded in an officer's notebook) in the absence of an appropriate adult unless the provisions of Annex C of Code C apply. If an urgent interview is authorised, and guidance requires the authorising officer to exercise his discretion only in exceptional circumstances, questioning may not continue once sufficient information to avert the immediate risk of serious harm has been obtained (Annex C, paras. 11.1 and 11.14 and Annex E, para. 8).

2.6.8 When present at an interview the appropriate adult must be informed by the police that he is not expected to act simply as an observer but that the purpose of his presence is:

(a) to advise the person being interviewed;

(b) to observe whether or not the interview is being conducted properly and fairly;

(c) to facilitate communication with the person being interviewed.

2.6.9 The case of *R. v. Aspinall*, referred to in para. 2.4.4, emphasised the importance of the various duties of an appropriate adult at the police station. In particular the court held that 'an appropriate adult was necessary to provide protection for the suspect and to discharge the duties set out in the Codes.' The court drew attention to Notes for Guidance, para. 11B which sets out the special care that should be taken by the police in interviewing vulnerable suspects and stressed the purpose for which the appropriate adult is required to attend and assist during the interview.

2.6.10 The appropriate adult must be present at charging or any other such action, e.g. bail to return or caution. A copy of the charge sheet must also be given to him.

2.7 The role of, and examination by, police surgeon/forensic medical examiner

2.7.1 Forensic physicians are independent from the police. In the United Kingdom they are referred to as police surgeons whereas in London they are known as Forensic Medical Examiners and in

Northern Ireland as Forensic Medical Officers. The PACE Codes of Practice refer to them as police surgeons and this term is adopted throughout this book.

2.7.2 Most police surgeons are general practitioners who are individually appointed under a contract to provide services on a rota basis for their relevant police authority. Each medical practitioner is a member of a group with a principal who is responsible for drawing up the rota and who receives an additional fee for this appointment. Police surgeons' fees depend on the nature of the call and time of day or night they attend the police station. They also receive an annual retainer. After three years they can take the Diploma in Medical Jurisprudence which entitles them to an additional annual fee. This qualification is not compulsory although it is becoming a contractual requirement by some employing police authorities.

2.7.3 Most police surgeons do not have any additional training to do the job, as at present only the Metropolitan Police have compulsory training courses and a requirement that the surgeon spends an eight-week attachment to a 'principal' prior to appointment. While all general practitioners will have spent six months working in a psychiatric hospital as part of their training when a senior house officer, and have received some training on identifying and treating psychiatric illnesses, they have no higher training in this area.

2.7.4 The police surgeon can provide one of the required medical recommendations for compulsory admission under the Act even if he is not a registered medical practitioner under s.12 of the Act (approved by the Secretary of State as having special experience in the diagnosis or treatment of mental disorder). However, the Mental Health Act Codes of Practice (para. 2.29) do advise that if he has no previous acquaintance with the patient, it is desirable that he be 'approved'.

2.7.5 As stated in para. 2.4.5, it is the responsibility of the custody officer to call the police surgeon to the station to examine the detainee. It is not expressly stated in the Codes who should or should not be present when your client is examined. If you are of the view that your client's best interests would be served by having either the appropriate adult or yourself present, then you should discuss this with him and get his consent. You should then tell the

21

custody officer and police surgeon of your client's wish. If they raise any objection or refuse the request there is no reason why you cannot ask to see an Inspector and make your complaint known to him and/or have it noted on the custody record.

2.7.6 There are two reasons why it may be advisable for you to be present at your client's examination by the police surgeon. Firstly, the officer in the case is often present together with his notebook to record any useful bits of conversation and secondly, police surgeons have been known to ask wholly inappropriate questions, to which you may wish to raise objection. The police surgeon has a duty to record his clinical findings in the custody record or note in it where they are recorded. The custody record will also note the length of time your client was out of his cell for the examination. Book 86 is provided by most police stations for the police surgeon to record his examination and findings. He will not get paid unless he completes the book. He may also keep his own clinical notes and, if the examination is an issue in any subsequent proceedings, you should ask for disclosure of these notes when preparing your client's case.

2.7.7 If the police surgeon is unsure whether your client is fit to be detained or interviewed, he can refer him to a hospital for a full psychiatric examination. Some police stations have a visiting psychiatric team so he could refer him to that team. You should be aware that the police surgeon does not have to be an approved registered medical practitioner under s.12 of the Act (see para. 2.7.4 above), to make a recommendation for an emergency admission under s.4. There is no reason why he, together with an approved social worker or nearest relative, cannot sign section papers to admit your client to hospital.

2.7.8 If your client is taken to hospital for examination, the PACE clock stops until he returns. If he is subsequently detained by the hospital, the custody officer also has the power to bail him to return to the station at a later date.

CHAPTER 3
Advice and assistance prior to interview

3.1 Keeping a record

3.1.1 From receipt of the first telephone call to leaving the police station, it is extremely important that you keep a full written record of all conversations with the custody officer, officer in the case, police surgeon and appropriate adult as well as a full note of your client's instructions and any advice you give him. As in any criminal case, there is always a possibility that, if your client is charged, you may be required to give evidence at court or your notes may be required to support a bail application and it is essential that a full and accurate note of your attendance at the police station is kept.

3.2 Role and aim of the representative

3.2.1 Before representing a mentally disordered suspect in the police station, you should be familiar with Home Office Circular 66/90 (see Appendix 5). The purpose of the circular is to draw to the attention of the police and Crown Prosecution Service (amongst others) 'the desirability of ensuring effective co-operation between agencies to ensure that the best use is made of resources and that mentally disordered persons are *not* prosecuted where this is not required by the public interest.' It confirms that alternatives to prosecution, such as cautioning by the police, and/or admission to hospital, or support in the community, should be considered *first* before deciding that prosecution is necessary.

3.2.2 Your main aim is to ensure that your client is afforded all the rights under the PACE Codes of Practice pertaining to mentally disordered suspects and where possible, to prevent a prosecution or to delay the decision to interview or prosecute pending a full medical examination of your client. This should give you an opportunity to make representations either to the police or prosecuting authorities. Awareness of the law and circulars and other guidances will enable you to represent your client's interests.

3.2.3 You should also be familiar with the local services and facilities available for mentally disordered people. Psychiatric hospitals and services are managed by Health Trusts and they should be able to provide information about the psychiatric services in your locality. These facilities can include a dedicated psychiatric hospital with a mixture of closed and open wards or a general hospital with psychiatric wards. Your local hospital may, for example, operate a 24-hour crisis intervention service enabling people who are mentally ill to be assessed in hospital or in the community at any time of the day or night. NHS patients may also be sent to private psychiatric hospitals under contractual arrangements with Health Trusts which purchase their services. Patients who are able to pay private hospital fees may of course be admitted at their own request or via a GP.

3.2.4 There are also a number of regional or medium secure units which provide secure accommodation for patients whose behaviour constitutes a risk to others. The average length of stay in these units is 18 months to two years and people often come to these units via the courts. There are currently three special hospitals, Ashworth, Broadmoor and Rampton, which provide treatment under conditions of maximum security for patients subject to detention under the Act. To be detained at a special hospital the patient must exhibit 'dangerous, violent or criminal propensities' (National Health Service Act 1947, s.4).

3.2.5 All hospitals operate a catchment area requirement and so it is important therefore to know where your client lives or, if homeless, last lived. Occasionally the place where the alleged offence took place is used to identify the appropriate catchment area. Information regarding out-patient facilities such as mental health hostels, day centres and drop-in centres can be obtained from your local social services department, as well as local advice agencies or MENCAP or MIND office.

3.3   Initial referral

3.3.1 Your initial request for advice is likely to come from one of the following sources:

(a) a relative/guardian of the detainee;

(b) the appropriate adult;

(c) the detainee (who may be an existing or former client);

(d) duty solicitor service;

(e) the detainee choosing from a list at the police station (Code C, Notes for Guidance 6B).

3.3.2 If the first telephone call is from someone calling on behalf of the detainee, e.g. a relative, take the basic details, i.e. name and address of detainee, date of birth, location of detainee, reason for detention, relationship to relative. If the issue of mental health has been raised by the person, ask for details of the nature and length of the illness, what treatment the person may be receiving or has received in the past and any current contact with a psychiatrist or social worker.

3.3.3 It is essential to speak to the detainee to confirm he wants you to act for him. If he does, obtain specific instructions on his mental health background, as your client must consent to you discussing this with the custody officer if the officer has not already received information to this effect. You must also ask your client if he consents to you continuing to communicate with the relative who made the initial contact and what information he authorises you to pass on to him.

3.3.4 If the referral is from the detainee via the custody officer, and the officer has confirmed that the person is being treated as mentally disordered under Code C, para. 1.4 and Annex E, para. 1, it may be helpful to ascertain the custody officer's 'lay' opinion on the nature and extent of your client's illness. If the police surgeon has already examined him, try and find out his opinion so that you have an idea how able your client is to speak to you on the phone and/or to give coherent instructions.

3.3.5 Always ask to speak to your client, as it is important to reassure him that you are independent from the police, his relative and/or the appropriate adult and to explain your role. If the issue of mental health has been raised you may wish to advise him that you are aware of some information relating to his mental health. If appropriate, try and obtain further information regarding current contact with mental health services, as it may be useful at an early stage to make contact with his psychiatrist, social worker or key worker. They may be able to provide you with more details of the nature and extent of your client's illness as well as the availability of care and treatment. If your client has stopped taking medication, they may be able to tell you how quickly the onset of symptoms will occur. You may also be able to obtain some guidance as to your client's ability to deal with a police interview. In order to provide this information the person will need to be satisfied that he has your client's express consent to disclosure.

3.3.6 It is extremely important that you act immediately if you are aware that your client is at risk of harming himself. If he is an established client and has a background of suicide attempts, it is vital that you tell the custody officer so that your client is kept under frequent observation by the police and any items in his possession are removed to prevent self-harm. If you are dealing with a new client, it is advisable when first talking to him on the telephone to ask him if he has a history of self-harm (e.g. wrist cutting) or attempted suicide. You will need your client's authority to pass on this information to the police. If he is reluctant to give it, explain to him that the fact he is considered a risk to himself will not in any way prejudice the police investigation but rather should ensure that he receives the appropriate care and treatment during his detention. If your client mentions harming others you should consider your position in accordance with the Law Society's guidance detailed at para. 3.5.3.

3.3.7 Your initial advice on the telephone should be to tell your client not to speak to the police about anything to do with the suspected offence or to sign any document (including the officers' incident report books) until you attend the police station. If the appropriate adult is already at the police station or may arrive before you, you *must* advise your client not to discuss details of the case with him. Due to the difference in rules on confidentiality, any admission to the offence made in the presence of the appropriate adult may be passed on to the police (see para. 3.5 below).

3.4 Arrival at the police station

3.4.1 On arrival at the police station, ask to see the custody record, as it will tell you whether or not your client has been examined by the police surgeon together with his opinion as to fitness to be detained and interviewed. If your client has not yet been examined, make sure the custody officer has telephoned the request for attendance of the police surgeon.

3.4.2 In the Metropolitan Police area, custody records include a continuation sheet entitled, 'Appropriate Adult and Medical Care' (Form 57M) which records the need for an appropriate adult and the need for medical attention. At the end of the form it is noted that regardless of the answers, if there is any doubt about the arrested person's medical condition, action to secure medical attention should be taken in accordance with Code C s.9 and current Metropolitan Police Service policy.

3.4.3 Check with the custody officer that the conditions of detention are appropriate. Although the Codes of Practice advise only that a juvenile should not be placed in a cell, if your client is being held in a cell and this is affecting his mental well-being, you should make representations to the custody officer that he be transferred to a detention room or some other more suitable accommodation. You should particularly make these representations if your client has a history of self-harm or attempted suicide as the Code also advises that people at risk should be visited in their cell (or other place of detention) more frequently than the mandatory hourly visits for other detainees.

3.4.4 You should be aware of Code C, para. 8.2 and Annex E, para. 13, which note that particular care must be taken when deciding whether to use handcuffs to restrain a mentally disordered or handicapped person in a locked cell. Make sure also that if your client requires any medication the custody officer is aware of this and has consulted with the police surgeon prior to the use of the medication (Code C, para. 9.5).

3.5   Conflict of roles and confidentiality: solicitor and appropriate adult

3.5.1 When the appropriate adult arrives at the police station, it is important that you spend some time with him before seeing your client to make sure that he understands his role as appropriate adult. Your discussions will vary depending on whether the appropriate adult is a professional, e.g. social worker, or a lay person e.g. relative or person appointed from a local panel of appropriate adults.

Social worker

3.5.2 Guidance issued to social workers acting as appropriate adults, advises them to see the detainee alone and *before* he sees his legal representative so that they can explain the difference between the role of the appropriate adult and the solicitor and they can explain that an admission of guilt to them may be passed on to the police. The British Association of Social Workers' Code of Ethics states that the social worker:

> '*recognises that information clearly entrusted for one purpose should not be used for another purpose without sanction. He respects the privacy of clients and confidential information about clients gained in his relationship with them or others. He will divulge such information only with the consent of the informant except where there is clear evidence of serious danger to the client, worker, other person or the community, in other circumstances judged exceptional, on the basis of professional consideration and consultation.*'

3.5.3 The advice given to social workers contradicts that which the Law Society issued to solicitors in May 1993, entitled *Advising a Juvenile, Mentally Disordered or Mentally Handicapped Suspect in the Police Station when an Appropriate Adult is Present.* The full text of this guidance is set out in Appendix 7. The main recommendation is that due to the difference between the code of conduct of solicitors and social workers and to ensure that a suspect has the opportunity of confidential consultation with his solicitor, the suspect must *first* be advised by the solicitor *in the absence of the appropriate adult* about the risk of disclosure. One of the reasons for this is that your client is more likely than not to be vulnerable and possibly very disordered and so the early presence of a sympathetic appropriate adult may encourage them to make admissions they might later regret.

3.5.4 Not all social workers belong to BASW and so it is not always clear what code of ethics they adhere to, if any. Some local authorities issue their own guidance whereas others have no policy on confidentiality. In September 1988, The Department of Health issued guidance to all Directors of Social Services in a document entitled *Personal Social Services: Confidentiality of Personal Information*. It justifies disclosure of personal information to a request from a senior police officer, e.g. superintendent or above, if it can help 'to prevent, detect or prosecute a serious crime.' If you have any doubts as to the individual social worker's position were your client to either make admissions in his presence or make remarks indicating a possible to danger to other persons, ensure you discuss this with the social worker prior to him seeing your client.

3.5.5 The case of *R* v. *Brown* (CA, 21 May 1999) highlights the problem of a client admitting an offence to a social worker, believing that the information would go no further. Brown (age 17) was arrested for causing grievous bodily harm. At the police station he had an appropriate adult who was a social worker. She had been his supervisor appointed by his local Youth Justice Team for the previous eight months. She attended the police interview together with his solicitor. After the interview she was alone with the defendant and he admitted having committed the offence. She discussed the conflict between her duty of confidentiality to her client and her obligations to the public with her employers. Subsequently, she made a witness statement to the police recounting his admission. The Crown Court judge admitted her evidence. The Court of Appeal upheld the conviction holding that the admission could not be excluded under ss.76 or 78. It confirmed the trial judge's finding that the duties of social workers with regard to confidentiality are not relevant to the question he had to decide. It found that the fact that the defendant did not realise that the confession would be used against him did not render its admission in evidence unfair.

Other professionals

3.5.6 Other professionals may be given guidance by their own professional body, for example if the appropriate adult is a nurse, or it may be set out in their contract of employment. However, they may have no guidance at all as to whether they owe a duty of confidentiality to the suspect. It is important that you discuss with the appropriate adult your different roles and find out their own view as to what they would do if your client were to make admissions in their presence.

Lay person

3.5.7 If the appropriate adult is a non-professional, e.g. a relative, they owe no duty of confidentiality to the suspect. You should carefully explain the role of appropriate adult to the person appointed, particularly in relation to the interview, that he is not there to persuade your client to answer questions but rather to safeguard his welfare during the interview.

3.5.8 Code C, Notes for Guidance 1B, states that when a police officer is investigating an offence, he is entitled to question any person from whom he thinks useful information can be obtained and further that all citizens have a duty to help police officers to prevent crime and discover offenders. If, therefore, a lay appropriate adult has received an admission of guilt the police could use this as evidence in any future prosecution. A recent example of this is the case of Fred and Rosemary West who were both arrested and charged with numerous murders and assaults. Fred West had a non-professional appropriate adult at the police station. Before trial he committed suicide. At his wife's trial, the appropriate adult was called to give evidence against her. This evidence was information obtained from her conversations with Fred West when acting as his appropriate adult.

Solicitors

3.5.9 The guidance for solicitors in respect to confidentiality is set out in *The Guide to the Professional Conduct of Solicitors 1999* Chapter

16 and Annex 16A, published by the Law Society. The overriding principle is one of absolute confidentiality 'save in truly exceptional circumstances.'

3.5.10 At para. 16.02 of the *Guide*, solicitors are advised that they may reveal confidential information to the extent that the solicitor believes it necessary to prevent the client or a third party committing a criminal act that the solicitor believes on reasonable grounds is likely to result in serious bodily harm. The Society further advises that in considering what might constitute exceptional circumstances, a solicitor must consider what would be in the public interest. The *Guide* states that the solicitor may only have a discretion to disclose confidential information to an appropriate authority in cases where he believes that the public interest in protecting children at risk outweighs the public interest in maintaining the duty of confidentiality.

3.5.11 If, having considered the facts of your particular case, you take the view that you may be entitled to disclose confidential information received from your client, you should first consider if there is any other way of remedying the situation without revealing the information and second, if the information is or is not disclosed whether you would be able to justify your actions to the Office of the Supervision of Solicitors or to a court. A non-solicitor should always consult their principal on the appropriate course of action to take.

3.5.12 The guidance issued to solicitors representing patients at Mental Health Review Tribunals (issued by the Law Society's Mental Health and Disability Sub Committee) is similar and also advises solicitors that if clients disclose to the solicitor that they intend to do serious harm to themselves or to someone else, guidance should be sought from the Law Society's professional ethics division. If they advise disclosure, you should still try and obtain the client's agreement to disclose. If that is not forthcoming, you must tell your client that you have been professionally advised to pass on the information and that it is better that you cease to act. Obviously, if you are in a police station outside normal working hours you will not be able to obtain telephone advice and will have to make the decision yourself taking into account all the factors set out above.

3.6   First consultation with the client

3.6.1   Prior to taking instructions from your client, ask to speak to the officer in the case. Find out the facts of the case and ask for disclosure and/or the opportunity to read any witness statements. If your client is being treated as a mentally disordered person (under Code C, para. 1.4 and Annex E, para. 1), it may be useful to obtain the officer in the case's view on the seriousness of the alleged offence and whether your client's mental health has any bearing on the commission of the offence. Ask if your client is to be interviewed and the way the officer sees the case progressing, e.g. taking no further action, caution, diversion or charge.

3.6.2   When acting for a client who is mentally disordered you may be required to consider your own personal safety. Occasionally the custody officer will raise this with you if he has been told by someone else or has himself experienced that the detainee may be violent or has indicated that he may harm someone. If you know the client then you may be in a position to assess the likelihood of danger to yourself if you are aware of his previous psychiatric history and diagnosis. If, on the other hand, he is a new client, you should be careful and ask the custody officer to allow you facilities to take instructions which are within eyesight or hearing of a police officer. In the latter situation you should safeguard the confidential nature of a solicitor–client interview and ensure that the officer is within calling range rather than able to hear your consultation with your client. You should specifically ask that any room/cell used by you should not be locked.

3.6.3   Your first consultation with your client should be without the appropriate adult for the reasons set out in section 3.5. Try to establish a rapport with your client as quite often people suffering from mental disorder have a distrust of professionals or people in authority. Explain the difference between your role and that of the appropriate adult and specifically ask your client at what point he would like the appropriate adult to be present. Your client may feel happier going through all the preliminary matters with you alone and you can then bring in the appropriate adult at the end to meet your client and explain his role in the proceedings.

3.6.4 Check with your client whether he would like anyone else informed of his arrest, such as a relative. This is a right which people with mental health problems or learning difficulties often do not take up on arrival at the police station, yet it can be of great assistance both to you and your client to speak to someone who knows him well. It may also help to alleviate any anxieties your client may have regarding the welfare or care of his children or other dependants.

3.6.5 If, during your private consultation, your client admits to a history of mental illness and even that he is currently receiving treatment but specifically tells you not to inform the police, you must abide by these instructions. If you are strongly of the opinion that it is not in your client's interests to withhold such details from the police then there could be a conflict of interest. Before deciding whether you should withdraw from the case, you should consider involving someone else to talk the matter over with you and your client. This could be a relative or the appropriate adult who might be able to help you persuade your client that informing the police would afford him more protection in the police station and be of advantage to him in the long term. If you are unsuccessful in changing your client's mind, you should explain to him that you are no longer able to act and that you will inform the custody officer that you are no longer representing him, without, of course, giving the officer the reason.

3.6.6 Depending on how ill your client is, you should try and take instructions with reference to the detailed checklist in Appendix 3. You should also have access to the *Pocket Reference*, which forms part of *Police Station Skills for Legal Advisers* published by the Law Society (London 1996). There is a helpful checklist of signs you should look out for when assessing your client's mental state and abilities. This checklist is also helpful if you are dealing with a client whose behaviour during the course of the interview alerts you to the fact he may have mental health problems. It is sometimes difficult to recognise, for example, a depressed mood, unless you are familiar with someone's normal behaviour.

3.6.7 Try and assess your client's mental disorder. This should become apparent to you when talking to your client, for example, he may not be able to concentrate for very long or may display paranoid ideas. If your client has stopped taking his prescribed medication, he may be experiencing new symptoms since stopping, making it difficult to communicate with you. Ask him whether he stopped with the knowledge of his treating doctor and when he had his last dose.

3.6.8 Research has revealed that a significant number of suspects detained in police custody are below average intelligence (Gudjonsson *et al.*, 1993; Lyall *et al.*, 1995). Clients whose learning difficulties fall within the definition of mental handicap are to be found among them. It can often be difficult for the legal representative (and the police and police surgeon) to identify a client with mental handicap. He may be able to complete simple tasks easily (e.g. signing your Legal Aid forms) while finding complex and stressful situations requiring rapid thought and articulate response (e.g. the police interview) beyond his ability. He is unlikely to volunteer that he has specific difficulties, and is less likely than a mentally ill person to have an active programme of mental health or social care.

3.6.9 If your client falls within the definition of mental handicap, he is likely to have problems with comprehension and expressing himself. Some people with learning difficulties can experience difficulty recalling information as they may take longer to take in information as well as understand and categorise it. Some find it difficult to record details and remember events in a form that can be understood by others. Limited language ability can result in some people with learning difficulties having problems in understanding a question or conveying precisely what they mean to say. Further research by Gudjonsson and others has revealed other difficulties including feeling intimidated during interactions with people in authority.

3.6.10 It is important that in every case, care is taken to discover exactly what form the disability takes so that by careful questioning, your client can give a reliable and complete account of events. When inquiring, for example, about your client's educational background to establish whether he attended a special school, do so with appropriate sensitivity. If you have doubts about his ability to read or write, you should satisfy yourself by direct evidence, e.g. by asking the client to read something. The Royal College of Psychiatrists and St George's Hospital have produced a series of booklets, Books Beyond Words, which explain police and court procedures to people with learning difficulties through pictures. The Home Office has encouraged the police to have the booklet called *You're under Arrest* available at police stations.

3.6.11 If relevant, warn your client that the police may wish to take fingerprints or DNA samples and explain the procedures for doing so. By forewarning your client it should reduce any anxiety he may have as well as preparing him for this step in the investigation.

3.7 Examination by police surgeon/psychiatric team

3.7.1 By now you ought to be able to assess whether your client needs a full psychiatric examination before the investigation proceeds any further. If you are of the opinion that this would be in your client's interests, get his authority for you to liaise with the police surgeon with a view to discussing this option with him. If he has already been examined by the police surgeon, you can ask the custody officer to recall the police surgeon to the police station if you are of the view that your client needs a further and more detailed examination and assessment.

3.7.2 If the police surgeon agrees with you, your client will usually be taken by the officer in the case to the local hospital for a psychiatric assessment. There is no provision in the PACE Codes of Practice for the appropriate adult to go with the detainee and so you should ask your client whether he would like the appropriate adult to attend with him. If he does, remember to advise your client not to discuss the case with the appropriate adult or accompanying police officers. In some areas of the country, police stations have arrangements with their local hospital whereby one or more members of the psychiatric team will attend the police station to make the assessment.

3.7.3 There is no obligation on your client to agree to being examined by a police surgeon or psychiatrist. Under General Medical Council guidelines entitled *Seeking Patients' Consent: The Ethical*

Considerations (published February 1999), a doctor is required to obtain the person's valid and informed consent to examination. Doctors are advised that no one can give or withhold consent on behalf of a mentally incapacitated patient and the doctor must first assess the person's capacity to make an informed decision about the investigation/treatment. Police surgeons should therefore obtain your client's consent both to the examination and to the release of his notes to the police, (often in the form of a section 9 statement), before the examination commences. In practice this is rarely done and, as such, is open to challenge.

3.7.4 If patients lack capacity, provided they comply, the doctor may carry out any investigation or treatment (which may include treatment for mental disorder) that the doctor judges to be in their best interests. If your client does not comply, the doctor may only compulsorily treat him for any mental disorder within the safeguards laid down by the Act. If you are of the opinion, however, that it is in your client's interests to be examined, because, for example, it might result in his being diverted and not being charged, then you should explain to him the benefit of such an examination.

3.7.5 Doctors (including psychiatrists) have a different duty of confidentiality from solicitors if they receive certain information during the course of a medical examination. The General Medical Council has issued a booklet entitled *Confidentiality* (published October 1995) containing their guidance on this subject. Doctors are advised that they must respect requests by patients that information should not be disclosed to third parties, save in exceptional circumstances. These include where a failure to disclose information may expose the patient, or others, to risk of death or serious harm and where disclosure is necessary for the prevention or detection of a serious crime.

3.7.6 Most police surgeons are aware of the difficulty it places them in if a suspect does start to confess to a crime or admit to thoughts of harming someone else and take steps to avoid being put in this situation by not asking leading questions. This problem may also arise at hospital when an examining doctor is making a psychiatric assessment at the request of the police.

3.7.7 In the case of *R. v. McDonald* [1991] Crim LR 122, the defendant, who was charged with murder, was examined by a psychiatrist for the purpose of determining fitness to plead, diminished responsibility and mental state in general. The doctor asked him about a piece of non-medical evidence and the defendant gave a reply which constituted an admission of the offence. The doctor's evidence on this point was allowed at his trial and he was convicted. Counsel for the defendant, in the Court of Appeal, conceded that the communication between the defendant and the doctor was not privileged and had not been obtained by oppression or inducement and further, that it was admissible for a doctor to give evidence on non-medical matters. The issue to be decided was whether the statement, once obtained, was used fairly. Earlier cases referred to by the court included *R. v. Payne* (1963) 47 Cr App R 80 and *R. v. Smith* (1979) 69 Cr App R 378, which held, *inter alia*, that there is no confidentiality in a doctor–patient relationship unless the defendant was expressly told that the content of the medical examination, for which his consent was required, would not be given in evidence.

3.7.8 These decisions need to be considered together with the GMC guidelines referred to at paras. 3.7.3 and 3.7.5 and the guidance issued to doctors who are preparing court reports. The latter is found in the Mental Health Act Code of Practice, para. 3.7 (see Appendix 6) which advises the doctor to explain the limits of confidentiality in relation to the report. Paragraph 3.11 specifically states that the report should not comment on guilt or innocence. There is absolutely no obligation on your client to discuss the alleged offence or any evidence with the doctor, as this is not essential to the examination and assessment at this stage. Your advice to your client must be not to discuss these matters so as to avoid these difficulties arising.

3.7.9 If you are of the opinion that your client is not fit to be detained or interviewed, it is worth discussing your view with the appropriate adult to enlist his support. If the police surgeon disagrees with you and certifies him fit to be detained and interviewed, you should make your representations known to the custody officer. The appropriate adult should be encouraged to do the same. If that fails you must address your representations to an Inspector and have your objections noted on the custody record.

Unfortunately, once a police surgeon has deemed your client fit to be detained and interviewed, the police invariably go ahead with an interview. A client may be fit to be interviewed and detained but still be vulnerable and it is important that both you and the appropriate adult are alert to his particular difficulties. See chapter 5 below as to what to do in the interview in these circumstances.

3.7.10 If you have any worries or doubts about the seriousness of your client's illness you should try and speak to his treating doctor, social worker or relative who knows him well as they may be able to advise you how your client was the last time they saw him and the nature of his illness. Code C, para. 9.4 expressly states that a detainee may, in addition to being examined by the police surgeon be examined by a medical practitioner of his own choice at his own expense. If your client's doctor/psychiatrist is willing to attend, the disbursement can be claimed from the Legal Aid Board under the Legal Advice and Assistance at Police Stations (Remuneration) Regulations 1989, SI No 342 reg. 5(4)(c). You will have to show that the disbursement was actually and reasonably incurred for the purpose of giving advice and assistance at the police station.

CHAPTER 4

Police interview

4.1 Taking instructions before the interview

4.1.1 Having made yourself familiar with your client's background, you must discuss with him the details of the prosecution case known to you. You should make clear to your client that the allegations are not yet proven and he has an opportunity to deny them in interview. It is particularly important that you should listen carefully to his instructions, giving plenty of time for the details to emerge and, if necessary, using the interviewing techniques set out in para. 4.2.7. You should check that you have recorded his instructions correctly in your notes by reading your client's account of events back to him. This consultation should not be in the presence of the appropriate adult for the reasons set out in para. 3.5 unless your client expressly wishes him to be present.

4.1.2 With mentally disordered suspects it is particularly important to consider all the elements of the offence, taking into account any subjective element which forms part of the *mens rea*. Your client's mental disorder may distort his understanding of events so that he has motives for his actions which are not based in reality or his mood may affect his judgement. You should record carefully any facts which, in his mind, amount to a defence.

4.1.3 Do not forget to ask your client whether he has answered police questions before your arrival or discussed the case with anyone else, e.g. the police surgeon or appropriate adult. This will prepare him for any question about a 'significant statement or silence' which may be put by police at the beginning of the interview in accordance with Code C, para. 11.2A. It will also prepare you for any intervention you may wish to make during the interview as to the admissibility of evidence.

4.2 Research on interviewing mentally handicapped people

4.2.1 Research confirms that the learning disabled are frequently vulnerable to making misleading statements in interviews (see especially Clare and Gudjonsson *et al.*, 'The vulnerability of suspects with intellectual difficulties during police interviews: a review and experimental study of decision-making,' 1995). There is a higher tendency among mentally handicapped people being questioned by police to go along with the story which is put to them, particularly if leading questions are put with a certain degree of force by the interviewer, which places pressure on the interviewee to comply.

4.2.2 The following tendencies have been noted in research:

(a) *acquiescence* i.e. the tendency to answer questions in the affirmative regardless of their content;

(b) *interrogative suggestibility*, i.e. a tendency either to be (mis)led by leading questions or to change initial answers in response to negative feedback from the questioner to the first response;

(c) *confabulation*, i.e. when people unconsciously replace gaps in their memories or add to existing memories with distorted or fabricated material. This is a less common, but still significant, tendency often driven by a desire to please the interviewer or to draw attention to oneself. This tendency is not thought to be associated with low intelligence so much as with personality abnormality.

4.2.3 It is common for the mentally handicapped suspect to believe that because he is being interviewed he must have done something wrong. The sense in which the interview is an investigation to establish the truth may escape him; thus he is less likely to put his version of events across in the face of opposition.

4.2.4 The desire to make oneself the centre of attention by confessing to serious offences, without regard to the consequences, may prey on the mind of some suspects. A well-known example of this is the case of *R. v. Ward* (1993) 96 Cr App R. Judith Ward, although of normal intelligence, suffered from a personality disorder. She 'confessed' to a large number of terrorist acts, some of which she could not possibly have committed, in order to bring 'interest and excitement to an otherwise lonely and friendless person', according to the psychologist Gudjonsson who gave evidence at her appeal. The same impulse, and the wish to be in a psychiatric hospital, led a defendant of limited IQ (73–6), to admit offences which he could not have committed (*R. v. Mackenzie* (1992) 96 Cr App R 98).

4.2.5 The wish to extricate oneself from the immediate situation and put an end to questioning was a feature in *R. v. Delaney* (1989) 88 Cr App R 338, in which a 17-year-old youth with an IQ of 80 was accused of sexual offences with a three-year-old girl. He initially denied the offences. During further questioning, the officers minimised the gravity of the offence and suggested to him that treatment, not punishment, was the likely outcome if he confessed, an approach they later justified by saying that they did not want to 'frighten him away from confessing his guilt'. The Court of Appeal allowed the appeal as unsafe and unsatisfactory remarking that the appellant was 'poorly equipped to cope with sustained interrogation and the longer the pressure was imposed on him the more confused he was likely to be in his own mind'.

4.2.6 Research into questioning witnesses who have learning disabilities has also shown that most are capable of giving reliable evidence, if the questioning is done in a way that they understand, and which does not encourage the tendencies to mislead set out in paras. 4.2.–4.2.5 above. Expert questioning of a mentally impaired suspect (or witness) can be a painstaking and lengthy process, requiring specialist knowledge and an awareness of the particular interviewee's difficulties. Ideally, the interviewer should have professional training and a full history of the interviewee before starting the interview. In the police station setting, this is not possible for the solicitor, appropriate adult or police officer.

4.2.7 The following suggestions are based on research into questioning witnesses who have learning disabilities (see especially the research paper by Bull and Cullen, *Witnesses who have Mental Handicaps*, 1992, (the Crown Office, Edinburgh 1992). You should adopt these in taking instructions and ensure, as far as possible, that they are followed by police in the interview.

(a) Questions which demand only a 'yes' or 'no' answer should be avoided. People with learning disabilities frequently give the answer 'yes' wrongly, in a misguided attempt to 'help' the interviewer by falling in with his version of events, or to disguise the fact that the question has not been understood.

(b) Avoid 'upgrading' answers which have been given by your client, for example, by repeating back to him what you understand him to have said, even though it was incomplete and unclear. He may acquiesce in the new version of events and a crucial element of the story may be lost. Do not finish sentences for your client even if he is struggling to express himself. Patience is essential.

(c) Try to break down an inconsistent answer into simpler phrases. If an answer is confusing and attempts to clarify it do not seem to work, leave it and move on. Insistence may easily force your client into a false agreement; returning to the question later when the sense of pressure has lessened may allow him to offer more detail.

(d) Be aware that many learning-disabled people find it difficult to describe emotion with any clarity, especially the emotions of others. Concepts such as shame, surprise and anger may be hard for them to convey in words. Concentrate on descriptions of events if possible.

(e) Avoid leading questions where possible. This should reduce the risk of acquiescence.

(f) Legal terminology and difficult words should be avoided wherever possible. You cannot avoid explaining certain legal terms to your client, for example, the caution. Similarly, it is unwise to assume that your client correctly understands common words, such as bail or custody. You should check that he understands these terms by asking him to explain them to you.

4.3 Advice before the interview

4.3.1 Having satisfied yourself that you have an accurate account of events with which your client agrees, you must consider, as with any client, whether he should answer police questions.

4.3.2 As a starting point, when considering whether to advise your client to remain silent, the criteria set out by Cape with Luqmani in the book *Defending Suspects at the Police Station* (LAG, 1999) p. 194, should be considered:

- knowledge of the police case;

- apparent strength of the evidence;

- admissibility of the police evidence;

- legality of the arrest, detention and questioning;

- prior comments and/or 'significant silences' of the client;

- likely fairness of the interview;

- apparent intelligence of the client;

- apparent mental condition of the client;

- apparent physical condition of the client;

- strength of the client's defence;

- any reason for early statement of the client's defence;

- specific reasons for remaining silent (e.g., to protect others);

- possible advantages of early admission of the offence(s).

4.3.3 Whether you advise your client to answer questions in interview depends on the facts of each individual case (as with any other criminal client) but you must always weigh up the nature and severity of your client's illness and ability to deal with and understand the questions in the interview against the result you hope to achieve for him.

4.3.4 You must consider whether the decision to advise your client not to answer questions will lay him open to the drawing of an adverse inference under s.34 Criminal Justice and Public Order Act 1994, drawing on the guidelines laid down in *R. v. Condron* [1997] Crim LR 215, and *R. v. Argent* [1997] Crim LR 346. In *Argent*, the court stated that a subjective test must be used for interpreting the circumstances which led to the client not answering police questions at the time. 'Circumstances' could include matters such as the time of day, the client's age, experience, mental capacity, state of health, sobriety, tiredness, knowledge, personality and legal advice. References to the accused meant to the actual accused with such qualities, apprehensions, knowledge and advice as he was shown to have had at the time. Clearly, if you decide that it is not appropriate for your client to answer questions, you must make a comprehensive record of all the factors which have led you to that decision.

4.4 Preparation for interview

4.4.1 Having taken full instructions from your client, you must explain to him the purpose of the interview about to take place. It is crucial that your client understands that evidence given in interview will form part of the case against him and that giving police the answers they seem to want is not necessarily in his interests in the long term.

4.4.2 You should go over the conduct of the interview with your client so that he understands the routine procedures. He should be told about the people who will be in the interview room, the taping of the interview, and the fact that his answers have to be audible. Explain to him that, although you are there to help him, he will have to answer the questions by himself and that you cannot speak for him. He should be told that at any time during the interview he can ask for it to be stopped if he wants to speak to you privately. Tell him that you and/or the appropriate adult will be able to intervene if necessary.

4.4.3 Practise an interview with him so that he is aware of how the interview will be conducted. It is also helpful to identify the likely questions he will be asked, *not* so that you can tell the client what answers to give but rather to assist him in understanding the question–answer format and to prepare him for the type and depth of questioning.

4.4.4 You must explain the caution to him and ask him to repeat it to you in his own words to ensure that he understands it. If you think he does not fully understand the caution, you should inform the custody officer and the officer in the case before the interview starts. You should also be prepared to justify your view during the interview. The officer may explain the caution in his own words if he thinks that the suspect does not understand it. (Code C, Note for Guidance 10C).

4.4.5 If you think your client is capable of being interviewed but may have problems understanding long words, inform the custody officer and the officer in the case. There may come a point when you ask for the interview to be stopped and it will be helpful to any argument that may arise later in court that you raised this at an earlier stage as well as intervened in the interview. It might be helpful to discuss your views with the appropriate adult to enlist his support if necessary. You should act in a similar manner if the appropriate adult conveys to you that he has doubts about your client's intellectual capacity.

4.4.6 Ask your client if he has any particular fears about the interview. He may be worried about something unconnected with the allegation against him, such as a child or a pet left unattended. You may be able to make arrangements which will put his mind at ease. He may be frightened of being bullied by police officers. You can reassure him that you and the appropriate adult will be with him throughout the interview and will raise any objections if this occurs. You should also explore at this stage what he expects to happen after the interview, to rectify any false impressions that he may have been given about bail.

4.5 The role of the solicitor in the interview

4.5.1 Mentally disordered offenders are unusually dependent on their solicitors' advice and protection during police interviews. You should protect your client at the interview stage, using all his rights under the Codes. It is unlikely that admissions made in interview will be excluded if he had a solicitor present (see *R.* v. *Dunn* at para. 5.4.1).

4.5.2 It is therefore necessary that you should be able to monitor your client's behaviour during the interview. Some police officers will try to sideline you into a passive role once the interview has started. You should make clear from the start that you intend to be active in your client's defence, in particular because of his vulnerability.

4.5.3 The seating arrangements in the interview room are important. If you find you are allocated a chair which is preventing you from having effective eye contact with your client so that you cannot monitor his state of mind, you should move it. Ed Cape (see para. 4.3.2) makes the helpful suggestion that if the officer objects to this, you should move your chair once the tape is running. The officer will find it much harder to challenge this while the tape is running, without sounding obstructive.

4.5.4 You should consider whether it will be helpful to your client for you to make an opening statement about your role at the beginning of the interview. It is a matter of practice and judgement in each case. If you are taking issue with the officer on a particular point, for example, that your client is unable to understand the caution, you will want to refer to this in your statement so that it is recorded on tape. If you have already made representations to the police that your client is unfit for interview, you should record it here as well as on the custody record. If you are advising your client not to answer questions for any reason, you should consider stating those reasons at this point.

4.5.5 You need to monitor your client's mental state throughout the interview. Mentally disordered interviewees are often able to answer questions easily at the start but can become confused or aroused as the pressure of being in a long interview begins to take effect. Your client may start to ramble incoherently or leave long pauses in his speech in such a way that you believe he may be responding to auditory hallucinations. If this occurs, you should consider stopping the interview with a view to making representations that he is not fit to be interviewed and requires further examination by a doctor.

4.6 Intervening during the interview

4.6.1 Code C, Note for Guidance 6D governs the solicitor's role in relation to his client when detained in the police station. It states clearly that the solicitor may intervene in order to seek clarification or to challenge an improper question to his client, or the manner in which it is put, or to advise his client not to answer particular questions or to give him further legal advice. It acknowledges that on occasion, this may require the solicitor to give advice which has the effect of his client avoiding giving evidence which strengthens a prosecution case. By Code C, para. 6.9 the solicitor may only be required to leave the interview if his conduct is such that the investigating officer is unable properly to put questions to the suspect.

4.6.2 The reasons for intervening, or for not intervening, in an interview must always be recorded in your written notes. You will have to give your reasons to the officer on tape, but you may wish to make fuller observations in your own notes which may be used later at trial.

4.6.3 The circumstances which require you to intervene will not differ essentially from those involving a client without any special vulnerability. In general these will be when you believe there has been a breach of PACE ss. 76–8 or the Codes of Practice or that the questions put are unfair either in form or content. Guidelines for police interviewers are set out in Home Office Circular 22/1992 'Principles of Investigative Interviewing', discussed in Ed Cape, *Defending Suspects at Police Stations* (LAG 1999), p. 295. He points out certain unfair approaches to questioning and eliciting confessions, including domineering and bullying questioning, topic hopping (jumping from subject to subject without allowing the suspect time to gather his thoughts), and seeking to persuade the suspect to answer questions by maximising the advantages and minimising the disadvantages of confession.

4.6.4 When representing a mentally disordered client, you should have a lower threshold of tolerance of any form of questioning which may fall into such categories. In particular, oppressive, bullying or pressurising interrogation is highly objectionable when used on mentally disordered suspects. Although, in *R. v. Emmerson* (1991) 92 Cr App R 284, the court found that rude and discourteous questioning with some shouting and bad language, was not oppressive within the meaning of s.76 (2), it might be so if it could be shown that the suspect's nature was such as to make him particularly easily overwhelmed by such behaviour.

4.7 The role of the appropriate adult in the interview

4.7.1 Code C, paras. 11 and 12, contain directions to officers on how to conduct the interview of any suspect. These paragraphs give specific directions on interviewing vulnerable or mentally disordered suspects, also summarised in Annexes C and E.

4.7.2 A mentally disordered or mentally handicapped suspect must not be interviewed or asked to provide or sign a written statement in the absence of the appropriate adult unless the provisions of para. 11.1 or Annex C of the Code apply.

4.7.3 Paragraph 11.1 permits emergency interviews of vulnerable suspects in the absence of an appropriate adult to be authorised by an officer of superintendent rank or above if delay would be likely:

(a) to lead to interference with or harm to evidence connected with an offence or interference with or physical harm to other people; or

(b) to lead to the alerting of other people suspected of having committed an offence but not yet arrested for it; or

(c) to hinder the recovery of property obtained in consequence of the commission of an offence.

4.7.4 An interview in the absence of the appropriate adult under the above provision may not continue once sufficient information to avert the risk has been obtained. Save in these circumstances the appropriate adult must also be present when the mentally disordered suspect is cautioned, and if not, the suspect must be cautioned again in the presence of the appropriate adult.

4.7.5 The appropriate adult must be present at the interview and must be informed of the provisions of Code C, para. 11.16 (Annex E, para. 9):

> '*Where the appropriate adult is present at an interview, he must be informed that he is not expected to act simply as an observer, and also that the purposes of his presence are, first to advise the person being questioned and to observe whether or not the inter-*

view is being conducted properly and fairly, and, secondly to facilitate communication with the person being interviewed.'

4.7.6 People acting as appropriate adults may interpret these guidelines in different ways and it is important to discuss them with your client's appropriate adult before the interview begins. If the appropriate adult is a professional, e.g. a social worker, he should be familiar with the process of 'facilitating communication with the client', which means enabling your client to tell his version of events as effectively as possible. It is not the appropriate adult's role to interpret this part of the Code of Practice as meaning that he is in a position to put pressure on your client to talk in the interview. Nor should he influence your client to alter his account. If possible you and the appropriate adult should agree what your respective roles are in the interview so that you do not intervene at the same time, which may confuse your client. For example, you could agree that the appropriate adult will intervene on issues related to your client's health and welfare, while you will intervene if necessary on legal issues.

4.7.7 Some non-professional appropriate adults, for example, family members, appear to think that part of their role is to press the client into making an admission. If you think this may be the case, you must stress to the appropriate adult that it is for you to give advice on legal matters – their role is to ensure that your client is not too distressed or under too much pressure in the interview. It will not be helpful to your client or his case if you and the appropriate adult are in conflict during the interview so you should make your respective roles clear before it starts.

4.7.8 Note for Guidance C11B and Annex Note E3 confirm that if there is any doubt about a person's mental state or capacity, an appropriate adult should be involved. It states that:

> *'people who are mentally disordered or mentally handicapped are often capable of providing reliable evidence, they may, without knowing or wishing to do so, be particularly prone in certain circumstances to provide information which is unreliable, misleading or self-incriminating. Special care should therefore always be exercised in questioning such a person.'*

Due to the risk of unreliable evidence it is important to obtain corroboration of any facts admitted where possible.

4.7.9 This note is crucial to the conduct of the interview of vulnerable people. It is both the role of the appropriate adult and the solicitor to ensure that the officer is aware of the suspect's particular difficulties and that special care is being exercised throughout the interview.

CHAPTER 5

Breaches of the Code of Practice in interview

5.1 Legal framework

5.1.1 PACE Code of Practice, Code C, paras. 11 and 12 and the Notes for Guidance cover the conduct of interviews of mentally disordered or vulnerable suspects. These provisions are brought together in Annex E of the Code, which is reproduced in Appendix 4 of this book. Breaches of these provisions form the basis of applications at trial to exclude evidence under ss.76–8 PACE. Applications to exclude evidence, in particular, interviews of mentally disordered suspects conducted by police in the absence of the suitable safeguards, are usually based on a combination of the grounds set out in ss.76–8.

5.1.2 Section 76 (2) PACE provides that the court must exclude any confession if it was or may have been obtained:

(a) by oppression of the person who made it; or

(b) in consequence of anything said or done which was likely in the circumstances existing at the time to render unreliable any confession which might be made by the accused in consequence thereof, unless the prosecution can prove beyond reasonable doubt that the confession (notwithstanding that it may be true) was not obtained in such circumstances.

5.1.3 Section 77 of PACE provides that a jury must be warned of the special need for caution where a case against a mentally handicapped defendant rests wholly or substantially on a confession made in the absence of an independent person.

5.1.4 Section 78 of PACE states that in any proceedings the court may exclude any prosecution evidence if it appears, having regard to all the circumstances (including the circumstances in which the evidence was obtained) that the admission of the evidence would have such an adverse effect on the fairness of the proceedings that the court ought not to admit it.

5.1.5 These provisions of PACE aim to protect mentally disordered suspects in the police station, especially in the interview. You must be aware of the case law which demonstrates how inappropriate questioning of mentally disordered suspects, particularly mentally handicapped people, may lead them to give unreliable evidence. It will enable you to take instructions from your client productively and sensitively and to ensure that he gives an accurate account of events to police in the interview.

5.2 Mental handicap: case law

5.2.1 The following cases provide practical examples of the courts' responses to situations which arose during the interviews of mentally impaired suspects. Almost all cases turn on three key factors:

(a) the level of the suspect's intelligence;

(b) whether effective legal representation was available; and

(c) whether there was a helpful and alert appropriate adult.

5.2.2 The effective use of suitable expert evidence of the defendant's mental condition at the time of interview is crucial in such cases to demonstrate to the court precisely why the nature of your client's mental disorder and the circumstances of his interview made it unreliable, oppressive or unfair.

5.2.3 In *R. v. Cox* [1991] Crim LR 277, the defendant, who had an IQ of 58, was interviewed by police without an appropriate adult present and admitted a part in two burglaries. He was illiterate but signed the note of interview after it was read to him. During the *voir dire* the judge rejected the evidence of an officer who said he did not know that Cox was simple or backward. However, Cox himself admitted the burglaries in the course of the *voir dire*, leading the judge to admit the interview on the basis that it was likely to be true. The appeal was allowed on the ground that there had been a breach of the Code (absence of appropriate adult). The issue to be considered in relation to s.76 (2) is whether the breach of the Code makes the confession unreliable, not whether the contents of it are true.

5.2.4 *R. v. Silcott, Braithwaite and Raghip* (1991) The Times, 9 December involved the repeated questioning of a youth (Raghip) who had an IQ of 74, in relation to the murder of a policeman during riots at Broadwater Farm Estate. Allowing his appeal, the Court of Appeal, having heard evidence from Dr Gudjonsson in relation to his learning disability, stated that they were not attracted to the concept that the judicial approach to submissions under the Act should be governed by which side of an arbitrary line, whether 69 or 70, the IQ fell. They preferred to assess in each case what effect the learning disability might have on the suspect's conduct in interview.

5.2.5 In *R. v. Moss* (1990) Cr App R 371, CA a 'borderline' mentally handicapped suspect was kept in custody for seven days during which time he was interviewed nine times about alleged sexual offences against four young children, two of whom were his own. He was refused access to a solicitor for 36 hours and subsequently after his assigned solicitor withdrew, he was interviewed without an appropriate adult or solicitor. He denied all allegations until the fifth interview, when some admissions were made. After six days and in the eighth interview he made admissions which formed the only evidence against him at his trial. The trial judge directed the jury under s.77 that special caution should be exercised, but refused to exclude the interview evidence. The Court of Appeal held that the defendant's mental disability, the length of the period in custody, the prolonged police interrogation, the fact that no admissions were made until the fifth interview, and that no solicitor or independent person was present, made the conviction unsafe and unsatisfactory.

5.2.6 The defendant in *R. v. Campbell* [1995] Crim LR 157 was convicted of conspiracy to rob and murder. His first interview, in which he made significant admissions, took place without a solicitor. He was then examined by the police surgeon who said that he was mentally handicapped. In a subsequent interview with a solicitor and appropriate adult present, he denied the offences but indicated some involvement. Later, in another interview with only his appropriate adult present, he made further admissions. The judge refused to exclude any interview although it was accepted that there had been a breach of the Code because of the defendant's IQ. He found that the police had no reason to know of the handicap before the medical examination and that it was speculation to suggest that he would not have made admissions if he had had an appropriate adult and a solicitor with him. His findings were upheld on appeal.

5.3   Other mental disorders: case law

5.3.1 Very few reported cases deal with suspects suffering from an active mental illness at the time of charge.

5.3.2 In *R. v. Walker* [1998] Crim LR 211, a woman was charged with a knifepoint robbery. On arrival at the police station she said she was a heroin addict and was prescribed methadone and valium. When interviewed she admitted some elements of the offence and at trial there was an unsuccessful attempt to exclude the interview under s.76 (2)(b). The defendant gave evidence at the *voir dire* that she had smoked crack cocaine in the police station and was under its influence when interviewed. A psychiatrist called by the defence gave evidence that the woman suffered from a severe personality disorder and that this was likely to have made her admissions unreliable because she might elaborate on events without regard to the consequences and smoking crack cocaine was likely to exaggerate this tendency. There was no other medical evidence called at trial but the officer in the case said that her mental state appeared the same before and after she had allegedly smoked the drug.

5.3.3 The trial judge did not believe the woman's evidence and while accepting that she suffered from a personality disorder, did not believe that this, without evidence of low intelligence, would render the interview unreliable. The interview was admitted in evidence.

5.3.4 On appeal, the court accepted that if evidence of a personality disorder was accepted the true construction of the words 'anything said or done' in s.76 (2)(b) includes not just wrong doing by police, but also other circumstances including the defendant's mental condition. Although most reported cases dealt with suspects of low intelligence, nothing in those cases limited or defined the particular form of mental or psychological condition or disorder upon which a defendant could rely to show that his confession was unreliable and thus to be excluded.

5.3.5 Even though the decision in *R.* v. *Walker* was based on the defendant's personality disorder rather than her contention that she had smoked crack cocaine, it seems that any mental or psychological condition or disorder may call s. 76 (2)(b) into force, even where that disorder is self-induced by the use of illegal drugs. This is relevant to the 'heroin withdrawal' cases in which it is often claimed by the defence that admissions made to the police in interviews are 'unreliable' within the terms of s.76 (2)(b) because the defendant was suffering withdrawal symptoms during the interview and made admissions to get out of the police station as soon as possible.

5.3.6 The case of *R.* v. *Goldenberg* (1988) 88 Cr App R 285 held that self-administration of drugs (something done by the defendant) does not fall into 'anything said or done' in the terms of s.76 (2)(b). It assumes that the thing said or done is 'something external to the defendant . . . which is likely to have some influence on him'. However, in *R.* v. *Crampton* [1991] Crim LR 277, it was accepted that withdrawal state might be a potentially relevant circumstance which could render the evidence unreliable under s.76 (2)(b), despite the fact that it was self-induced.

5.4 The role of the legal representative: case law

5.4.1 The general approach of the courts has been that a defendant accompanied in interview by a legal representative is protected from oppression, unfairness and the other breaches of the Codes which ss.76–8 aim to prevent. In *R.* v. *Dunn* [1990] Crim LR 572, it was made clear that a lawyer is expected to intervene to prevent breaches of the Code and failure to do so, if justified at the time of interview, would deter the trial court from excluding evidence even if improperly obtained. There are rare cases in which a solicitor (with or without an appropriate adult) has been present at the interview but the court has found nevertheless that the confession evidence should be excluded.

5.4.2 One such case is *R. v. Paris, Abdullahi and Miller* [1994] Crim LR 361, known as the case of the 'Cardiff Three'. The defendant Miller, who was later discovered to have an IQ of 75, was subjected to interviews over five days which took up 19 tapes. In all but two of the interviews he was with a solicitor who, despite mounting bullying, shouting and pressure by police, did not intervene. Having denied involvement over 300 times, Miller made 'admissions' on tapes 18 and 19.

5.4.3 Allowing his appeal, the Court of Appeal criticised both the police, whose behaviour amounted to 'oppression' within the meaning of s.76 (2), and the solicitor. The police were wrong to assume that their behaviour was within the Codes because the solicitor did not intervene, but it was equally important that a solicitor assisting a suspect at interview should discharge his function responsibly and courageously, as otherwise his presence might actually render a disservice to the client.

5.4.4 In general the courts have treated the presence of a solicitor as being sufficient protection for the suspect in spite of the absence of an appropriate adult which constitutes a breach of Code C, para. 11.4. This makes it all the more essential that you are active in safeguarding your client's rights in the interview process.

5.4.5 In *R. v. Law-Thompson* [1997] Crim LR 675, a highly intelligent man suffering from an autistic spectrum disorder, Asperger's syndrome, was arrested for threatening to kill his mother with a meat cleaver. When cautioned he made admissions to police. A psychiatrist at the police station saw him and the police arranged for his social worker to attend. The social worker said that an appropriate adult was not necessary. The man was interviewed without an appropriate adult but with a solicitor. He admitted the offence in the interview.

5.4.6 An appeal based on s.76 (2)(b) failed on the basis that there was nothing to suggest that the confession was obtained because the appropriate adult was absent or that such absence was likely to render the confession unreliable. The court further confirmed that the judge's discretion under s.78 need not be exercised if there was nothing in the circumstances to suggest unfairness as in this case. Here the crucial factors were the presence of the solicitor, the intelligence of the defendant in spite of his abnormal social functioning and the independent evidence of his guilt.

5.4.7 Other cases (particularly *R.* v. *Lewis* (*Martin*) [1996] Crim LR 260) have suggested that although an appropriate adult may have greater insight into the difficulties of a person with a low IQ, the role of the appropriate adult and the solicitor during interview are essentially similar. This is to ensure that:

(a) the accused fully understands his rights;

(b) the interview is conducted correctly;

(c) the police do not abuse their position;

(d) the accused is able to make himself clearly understood; and

(e) he clearly understands what is being put to him.

5.4.8 In the *Lewis* case, the suspect had an IQ of 69 which was not recognised at the police station, nor raised at trial. Although a solicitor was present at the interview, no appropriate adult was called. The appeal was rejected because the confession, although obtained in breach of the Code, i.e. the absence of an appropriate adult, was not unreliable as a solicitor was present. However, the court criticised the solicitor for failing to obtain evidence of his client's mental disorder which must have been apparent to him by the time of trial since at the time of arrest he was on probation with a condition of psychiatric treatment.

5.5 The role of the appropriate adult: case law

5.5.1 Recent Court of Appeal cases, (*Aspinall* mentioned at para. 2.4.4) and *Haroon Ali* (see below) have emphasised the wide and active role of the appropriate adult in the interview process. In *Aspinall*, the court emphasised that a crucial aspect of their role is to ensure that 'special care' (as outlined in Note C11B) (see para. 4.7.8) is taken when interviewing a mentally handicapped suspect. The court also stressed that the function of the appropriate adult was to act as a 'gateway' to other safeguards, especially in advising the suspect when to obtain legal advice. The court's judgment appears to assume that the appropriate adult, unlike the solicitor, would have special training in dealing with mentally disordered or learning disabled people, an assumption not necessarily borne out in practice.

5.5.2 In *R.* v. *Haroon Ali* (CA, No 98/04160/X2) an 18-year-old was found in possession of 11 wraps of heroin. At the police station he was interviewed for nine minutes without an appropriate adult, having declined legal advice. He admitted possession with intent to supply, and two minutes into the interview further admitted supplying drugs on a large scale for the previous two years, giving details of high earnings, owning an expensive car and other extravagant claims. There was no other evidence against him except these admissions, but he was charged with possession with intent to supply and also three counts of supplying heroin over the previous two years.

5.5.3 By the time of trial it was established that the defendant's IQ range was between 66 and 72, although it was said that there had been nothing in the defendant's demeanour at the time of arrest and questioning to suggest this. Unsuccessful efforts were made at trial to exclude the whole interview on the basis that the defendant had been offered inducements by police to fabricate admissions as to his dealing activities. This submission was rejected after a *voir dire*. It was further submitted that conducting an interview with a mentally handicapped person without an appropriate adult present was in breach of Code C, para. 11.4 of PACE and the judge should therefore exercise his discretion to exclude the evidence under s.78 PACE.

5.5.4 The judge found that the defendant was indeed mentally handicapped and a breach of the Code had taken place, but not so grave as to lead automatically to the exclusion of the whole interview. He excluded the later admissions but found that the jury could safely accept the first part of the interview as reliable. The defence opted to put the whole interview into evidence, presumably to pursue the inducement defence. The defendant was convicted on all charges and appealed.

5.5.5 Allowing the appeal, the court said that the absence of an appropriate adult does not lead automatically to the exclusion of the interview record; each case and its circumstances must be considered individually. In this case, the court considered that, had an appropriate adult been present, there would have come a point when he would have 'intervened to establish from the defendant privately whether he really meant what he was saying, whether he was boasting and whether he wanted to suspend the interview so that a solicitor could give him further advice'. The defendant was aged 18 and was by that stage known to suffer from mental handicap. Admissions made in a very short interview in the absence of either an appropriate adult or a legal adviser were the sole evidence against him. The court found, under s.76, 'that the convictions (for supplying drugs) may not be safe because the defendant within that very short interview was giving answers which were possibly reliable but also answers which were likely to be unreliable and fanciful'.

5.5.6 This case provides a useful example of the active role now expected of an appropriate adult when intervening to prevent exaggeration and in advising when legal representation becomes vital.

CHAPTER 6
Assistance after the interview

6.1 Diversion

6.1.1 Your client can be diverted from being charged if the police either take no further action, give your client an informal warning or administer a caution. They can also bail your client to return to the police station at a later date while they obtain further medical advice or refer the matter to the CPS to decide whether prosecution is in the public interest.

6.1.2 The police can also liaise with other professionals to achieve voluntary or compulsory admission to hospital under the civil sections of the Act (see Appendix 2 for the full text of these sections). The only pre-requisites for informal admission are that the patient does not resist admission or continued residence in hospital and that the hospital managers and the care team have made a bed available based upon the person's need for care and treatment. Compulsory admission may be indicated even though your client is agreeing to informal admission to hospital. This is likely to occur if his current mental state, together with reliable evidence of past experience, strongly suggests that he will change his mind about staying in hospital voluntarily with a resulting risk to his need for treatment and/or safety of others.

6.1.3 The *Inter-Agency Working Document* (issued with Home Office Circular 12/95) sets out the criteria the police should apply when considering when to charge and thus whether your client enters the criminal justice process. The police are advised that the existence of mental disorder should never be the only factor considered in reaching a decision about charging. To reach a decision the police will need to find out whether your client has a history of mental disorder and/or any previous criminal convictions and take that background into account in assessing the need for action in order to protect the safety of the public.

6.1.4 You will be able to make representations to both the officer in the case and custody officer on whether or not your client should be charged. A lot will depend on the seriousness of the alleged offence and whether the incident can be shown to be an isolated event or whether it is part of a developing pattern of behaviour which may put the public at risk in the future.

6.1.5 If the police decide not to charge your client and take no further action, then that is the end of the matter. If your client has support in the community but does not take it up, there is no harm in you encouraging your client to cooperate with those concerned with his care, particularly if it will help to avoid further contact with the police.

6.1.6 If the police are willing to caution your client, it is important that you explain to him the full implications of the caution, including the fact that it will remain on his list of criminal convictions for five years and might be used against him if he finds himself in the same position again. Your client can only be cautioned if he understands the effect of his actions. This can sometimes cause difficulty with some clients and so you must also satisfy yourself that your client is able to comprehend that what he has done is wrong and that effectively he is being given an official 'ticking-off'. The appropriate adult must be present when the Inspector administers the caution.

6.1.7 If your client is bailed to return to the police station at a later date it can be for a number of reasons. The police may want to make further inquiries into the alleged offence or consult with the CPS as to whether your client should be charged or have your client examined by a psychiatrist to advise on his mental health. In the latter situation, your client is not obliged to attend such an appointment but it might be useful to do so, if it could result in his not being prosecuted. The same difficulty arises in relation to confidentiality as discussed in Chapter 3, para. 3.7.5. Your client may be asked questions about the offence and you should advise him, where possible, not to make any admissions or discuss the evidence.

6.1.8 You may also wish to instruct a psychiatrist to provide you with an opinion which you can then use to back up any representations to the police not to charge your client. If your client is currently receiving outpatient treatment then you should try and instruct his doctor. You will need to get your CLAIM 10 form extended to cover the cost of the report. When instructing the psychiatrist you should include many of the points set out in Chapter 7, in particular the effect a prosecution would have on your client's mental health and whether your client needs formal or informal treatment in hospital.

6.1.9 If the report is helpful, you should consider disclosing it (with your client's express agreement) to the police/Crown Prosecution Service with an accompanying letter highlighting the main points of the report which assist your representations to divert your client from the criminal justice process. You should always consider quoting the Home Office Circular 66/90 (see Appendix 5) on whether it is in the public interest for your client to be prosecuted.

6.1.10 If your client is to be admitted to hospital voluntarily or under a civil section of the Act, this can be done whether he is already at the hospital for a psychiatric examination or still at the police station. If the hospital where your client is being examined arrange the admission, then the custody officer can decide either to take no further action on the case or to bail your client to return to the station at a later date. There is no need for your client to be brought back to the station for this to be done.

6.2 Charge and bail

6.2.1 If the officer in the case is of the view that your client should be prosecuted, the matter will be referred back to the custody officer for a final decision. It is at this stage that you can make representations to the custody officer to try and persuade him/her not to charge your client. Factors to consider include the nature and seriousness of the offence, whether the behaviour put the public at risk, availability of and access to health and social services care and your client's record of compliance with treatment. If the custody officer decides to charge your client, this must be done in the presence of the appropriate adult who is also given a copy of the charge sheet.

6.2.2 Your client must be granted bail until his first appearance at court unless any of the following conditions apply:

(a) His name or address is unsatisfactory.

(b) Detention is necessary for his own protection or other people's protection or to prevent loss or damage to property.

(c) There are reasonable grounds to believe he would fail to appear in court or interfere with witnesses/evidence.

(d) In the case of an imprisonable offence, the custody officer has reasonable grounds for believing that the detention of your client is necessary to prevent the commission of further offences.

(e) If your client is also a juvenile, he can be detained in his own interests.

(s.38 (1) PACE 1984)

6.2.3 Bail can be granted subject to any conditions available to a magistrates' court save that the custody officer cannot bail someone to reside at a bail hostel. In cases involving mentally disordered suspects, the custody officer's usual objections are that your client may harm himself or others. If your client's current or previous behaviour appears to put others at risk, then it is unlikely he will be granted bail and he will be kept in custody to be produced at court the following morning. You must always address the issue of bail on behalf of your client as continued detention may exacerbate his mental disorder.

6.2.4 If your client is charged, it is advisable to complete legal aid forms for the magistrates' court hearing so that you can apply for legal aid as soon as possible.

CHAPTER 7

The first appearance in the magistrates' court

7.1 Appearing in the magistrates' court

Whether or not you have represented your mentally disordered client in the police station, you may find yourself acting for him at the first appearance in the magistrates' court. This may be as an 'own' or duty solicitor. Under the 'Narey' measures, the case is likely to be listed for an Early Administrative Hearing (EAH). If the client's mental disorder has not been recognised by police or his representative at the police station, it may be listed as an Early First Hearing (EFH) case.

7.2 Bailed to attend court

7.2.1 Legal aid – The Legal Aid Board (LAB) will pay a duty solicitor of choice to provide representation at an EAH or EFH or at an adjourned hearing provided the case remains within the EAH/EFH list. However, you will not be covered for work done between the hearings unless the client has signed a CLAIM10 form. In the circumstances you should apply for legal aid in the normal way. The *Legal Aid Handbook*'s guidance on criminal legal aid confirms that 'legal aid should be granted if the applicant is unable to follow proceedings or properly conduct his case by reason of ... mental disorder, mental impairment or subnormality'. You must at the same time obtain a written authority to disclose medical and social service records from your client. The grant of legal aid will enable you to apply, where appropriate, for prior authority from the LAB to obtain a psychiatric report. This will involve deciding what your strategy for the base will be having considered your instructions. See para. 7.3.1 below.

7.2.2 Taking instructions – At your first meeting with your client you will need to take, as far as circumstances allow in each case, full instructions including the details set out in the checklist (see Appendix 3). You should consider consulting, as appropriate and with your client's written authority, all or any of the following:

(a) RMO, past or present;

(b) social worker;

(c) key worker;

(d) CPN;

(e) hostel staff;

(f) probation officer;

(g) family.

7.2.3 When discussing a client's previous contact with mental health services, you will need to cover in detail:

(a) his history of compliance with treatment, both in hospital and in the community;

(b) the level of care in the community offered to your client;

(c) whether that support has been consistently offered;

(d) whether he has accepted it.

Clients often have a period of compliance after discharge from hospital followed by stopping medication and/or withdrawing from mental health services. This may lead to a deterioration in their mental state. If your client is currently being prescribed medication, you need to establish who has prescribed it, whether he says he is taking it, and if not, the reason why he has stopped. Frequently clients stop taking their medication because they believe they are 'better' and no longer need it or because they are suffering adverse side effects. You must establish whether your client is willing to recommence treatment and if so, whether an outpatient appointment can be obtained for him before the first hearing date.

7.2.4 If your client has withdrawn from mental health services, find out the reasons why. There may have been a change of CPN or social worker or a lapse or decline in the care offered.

7.2.5 Before obtaining a medical report or finding out whether your client needs to be re-admitted to hospital or receive further outpatient treatment, you should ascertain his attitude to hospital and medical treatment generally. As many clients are anxious to avoid any further treatment, you must make sure that he is willing for you to pursue a 'medical disposal' of his case. You must respect his instructions in this respect and resist colluding with the court to effect a disposal of the case which the client opposes, even if you feel it is in your client's best interests.

7.2.6 In addition to obtaining the normal advance disclosure, previous convictions and custody record, it is important to obtain a copy of the police surgeon's report if any and a copy of any s.136 documentation. You need to take your client's comments on these documents.

7.3 Strategy and options

7.3.1 You will need to consider at this stage whether you wish to obtain a medical report on your client. This will depend on your client's wishes and also on the probable outcome of the case as you see it. If diversion from prosecution is a possibility, taking into account the seriousness of the charge and other factors laid out in the Code for Crown Prosecutors (see para. 7.4.2), you will undoubtedly need to obtain a medical report, ideally before the case comes before the magistrates on the first occasion.

7.3.2 If the case is clearly not within the CPS guidelines for discontinuance, your decision on whether to obtain a medical report will depend on your client's likely plea and the purpose of a report in his case. In the case of a mentally impaired client, for instance, where his low intelligence may be a factor in the court's decision as to whether evidence should be excluded, a specialist report should only be obtained after you have full disclosure of the prosecution case. You should decide whether a report would be helpful before plea or after plea, and if so, for what purpose. You may need a report to ensure that your client receives treatment, for example if he is suffering from florid symptoms of schizophrenia. On the other hand it could be used to mitigate sentence, for example, in the case of a client with a history of depression who is receiving outpatient treatment.

7.3.3 In the case of a minor offence, an early plea of guilty may be preferable in terms of sentencing advantage, if for example, a conditional discharge is a possibility. In this case you might not wish to obtain a report before the first hearing. If this strategy fails and the case is adjourned for pre-sentence reports you can always reconsider whether a report would be helpful.

7.4 Instructing the doctor

7.4.1 If it is likely that you will be seeking long-term inpatient care you should seek a report from your client's existing or recent RMO or from the catchment area consultant with a view to finding a local bed for him. If he only requires outpatient treatment, the consultant will be able to confirm the services supplied by the local community outreach team. Even if your client is receiving treatment from a consultant, you may wish to obtain a report from an independent doctor for a second opinion on diagnosis and/or treatment. If your client has particular difficulties which require a specialist consultant, for example learning disability or sexual deviation, you will need to locate a consultant in that field. When a client is accused of a violent or sexual offence a full 'risk assessment' prepared by a forensic psychiatrist will be necessary. This should make a prediction about the risk of future danger based on all that is known about your client, his history, psychological make-up and current mental state.

7.4.2 The letter of instruction to the psychiatrist should be as detailed as possible particularly where the doctor has no prior knowledge of your client. It is essential to establish that the doctor will be able to see your client and write the report in good time so that if appropriate it can be submitted to the CPS for their consideration before the court date. If this cannot be done, you should seek an adjournment, giving reasons why the doctor's report is needed. You must also agree a fee for the report which is acceptable to the Legal Aid Board.

7.4.3 In addition to the usual details about the client, it may be helpful to include in the letter of instruction some or all of the following:

(a) client's address and type of accommodation (e.g. DSS hostel, bedsit);

(b) nature and background of the offence (if you are asking the

67

doctor to make a risk assessment, send him at least a copy of the victim's statement and whatever additional documents are available);

(c) brief social history of client including family or social support;

(d) previous convictions;

(e) medical history and history of treatment and compliance;

(f) client's instructions and wishes.

7.4.4 You should then ask the doctor to comment on the following:

(a) your client's mental state both at the time of examination and the time of the incident;

(b) whether there is a causative link between your client's mental state and the commission of the offence;

(c) whether your client is suffering from a mental disorder;

(d) whether he is fit to plead;

(e) whether he is suitable for a probation order with a condition of psychiatric treatment;

(f) whether there are sufficient grounds for him to be sectioned under the Act;

(g) if he advises that he should be admitted to hospital under section, find out if the doctor can effect his admission to hospital and will be able to arrange the second doctor's opinion necessary for detention under the Act.

7.4.5 If you are seeking a discontinuance of the case on medical grounds you should seek the doctor's opinion on the effect on your client's mental state if the prosecution were to continue. This is particularly important if your client has a history of self-harm or severe depression.

7.4.6 Chapter 3 of *Mental Health Act 1983 Code of Practice* (1999 edition) provides essential guidance to doctors preparing reports for the use of the court in relation to patients concerned in criminal proceedings. These guidelines should be followed by doctors asked by the court to prepare a report and also by those instructed by solicitors. The relevant paragraphs are set out at Appendix 6. If you have not instructed the doctor before to write reports for use in criminal proceedings, it may be helpful to send a copy of the guidelines with your letter of instruction.

7.5   The argument for discontinuance

7.5.1 Once the medical report has been obtained, you must discuss the contents with your client and obtain his authority to disclose it to the CPS if appropriate. The letter which accompanies the medical report should set out your reasons as clearly as possible and high-light passages in the report which are favourable to your client. Your letter ought to be considered by a Senior Crown Prosecutor and you may find it useful to speak to the Prosecutor concerned if you are of the opinion that you have a persuasive case. The CPS will often wish to consult police and witnesses in the case so they need to receive the representations in reasonable time before the hearing.

7.5.2 The particular criteria to be considered by the CPS as to whether the case should be discontinued are set out in para. 6.5(f) of the Code for Crown Prosecutors:

> '*A prosecution is less likely to be needed if . . . the defendant is or was at the time of the offence suffering from significant physical or mental ill-health, unless the offence is serious or there is a real possibility that it may be repeated. The Crown Prosecution Service where necessary applies Home Office guidelines about how to deal with mentally disordered offenders. Crown Prosecutors must balance the desirability of diverting a defendant who is suffering from significant mental or physical ill-health with the need to safeguard the general public.*'

7.5.3 Crown Prosecutors are reminded by the Code to apply the principles of Home Office Circulars, the most relevant being 12/95 and 66/90 (see Appendix 5).

7.5.4 Your arguments must follow these criteria and should show a realistic understanding of the seriousness of the offence and the likely sentence, as well as a regard for the victim (where relevant). If your client has previous convictions for similar offences or there is an apparent risk of repeat offences (for example offences involving neighbours, about whom your client has developed delusional beliefs) the question of future risk must be dealt with as far as possible. If it is clear that the offence was due to a short-term lapse in compliance with medication after a long period of stability in the community, and that the previous status quo can be or has already been restored, the argument for discontinuance will be strengthened.

7.6 In custody overnight to appear the following morning

7.6.1 This is likely to be the case where the offence charged is serious, particularly one of violence, or where your client's mental state or other circumstances suggest that he is likely to be a danger to himself or others or may not surrender to bail. In practice, mentally disordered clients in custody present the most immediate difficulties for representatives as the strategy of the case must be considered at the first appearance, although the considerations remain the same as those mentioned in para. 7.3 above.

7.6.2 Apply for legal aid. Although the LAB accepts that custody cases can be listed as EFHs or EAHs and thus you may attend court as duty solicitor of choice, it is advisable to apply for legal aid for the reasons set out in para 7.2.1. If you are dealing with a client who refuses to sign the forms due to their mental state, an application may be made in open court to the bench to waive the requirement for the defendant's signature. You will generally find the court is all too eager to grant legal aid where the client's mental state is very clear from his behaviour in court.

7.6.3 Members of the client's family may attend court. They can be an invaluable source of background information about your client, especially in the case of clients with learning difficulties. They can also offer practical support, for instance in connection with a bail application (see below, para 7.7). If treatment under the act is a possibility, it is advisable to establish the identity of your client's 'nearest relative' in the terms of the Act. Note however that frequently family members will have very strong and often justifiable concerns about your client's treatment by police and/or health or social services. They may well paint a much more serious picture of your client's illness, vulnerability or dangerousness than your client is prepared to accept. It is essential you adhere closely to his instructions and explain your professional role to his family.

7.7 Bail

7.7.1 The mentally disordered defendant has the same general right to bail under the Bail Act 1976 (with the normal exceptions under CJPOA 1994) as any other offender and the general presumption in favour of bail operates (s.4 (1), Bail Act 1976). However, you must consider not only the usual general objections under Sched. 1, Part 1, para. 2 (failure to surrender to bail, commission of further offences, interference with witnesses etc.,) but also whether the court may find that a remand in custody is necessary for the defendant's own protection (Bail Act 1976, Sched. 1, Part 1, para. 3). Before the case is called you should have explored thoroughly the various means of providing treatment to your client outside prison, either in the community or in hospital.

7.7.2 The bail conditions particularly appropriate to mentally disordered defendants may include:

(a) *Residence at home address.* The court may impose a condition of residence to ensure that the defendant stays in the community and receives outpatient treatment. You should find out what the arrangements are for regular visits by a CPN and/or social worker and if possible get them to increase the intensity of support during the period of remand, so that the court can rest assured that the defendant's mental state is being regularly monitored by professionals.

(b) *Keep appointments for medical treatment.* If your client is linked in with mental health services it may be helpful to fix an outpatient appointment with his CRMO while at court. The confirmation of such an appointment, attendance at which can be made the subject of a bail condition, may well assist you in a bail application, especially if a member of your client's family is willing to accompany him.

(c) *Co-operate with the preparation of a medical report.* If it is proposed that a report on the defendant's mental condition should be prepared during the remand period the court may use its power under s.3 (6), Bail Act 1976 to impose a bail condition to co-operate with the preparation of such a report. This power may be exercised at any stage of the proceedings. Consistent support from outside agencies will also be helpful to reduce the force of other objections to bail, especially commission of further offences and failure to surrender.

(d) *Remand to bail or other hostel.* Most bail hostels are unwilling to accept actively mentally ill residents, but hostels specialising in clients in touch with mental health services do exist. Key workers at such hostels are able to remind the client to keep appointments and take medication, and to monitor their mental health. In the case of people with learning disabilities who require a measure of social support and guidance, a highly staffed hostel may be an appropriate bail address. Assistance from the probation service and bail support schemes is usually essential to identify a suitable placement.

(e) *Remand to psychiatric hospital:*

    (i) Your client may be admitted to hospital on remand in a number of ways. If he is already an informal patient and the treating doctor agrees, a condition of residence may be imposed, requiring him to reside at a particular hospital. The court may wish to impose a specific condition that he remain on a particular ward (usually a locked ward), which has the effect of preventing the treating doctor from exercising his usual discretion to impose such conditions of security as are clinically appropriate.

    (ii) If during the period of remand to a hospital, the hospital want to discharge your client as no longer needing treatment, this will obviously place him in breach of bail. It is important to liaise regularly with the hospital to ensure that a bed is still available for your client before each remand date. If they wish to discharge him you should find out the arrangements made for his accommodation and after-care and the names and details of those who will provide it (social worker, CPN, etc.) to assist you in an application to vary his bail.

(iii) Your client may be admitted to hospital under a section of the Act, either a civil section (ss.2–3), or s.35, which permits the magistrates to remand a defendant to hospital for the preparation of a psychiatric report (see para. 7.12). Admission under section always requires the patient to be assessed by at least one psychiatrist before admission, either at the police station or at court through a mental health assessment scheme (also known as the court duty psychiatric scheme). Such schemes are discussed more fully below in para. 7.11).

7.8   Protection of your client and others

Protecting the suicidal client

7.8.1 Representing a client in custody who is expressing an intention to harm himself may place the advocate in a difficult and anxious position, particularly when there is no report available to the court and your client is likely to be refused bail. It is sometimes difficult to assess the seriousness of such threats and therefore all threats, whether explicit or implicit, must be taken seriously. The Prisoner Escort Record (PER) form accompanies all prisoners from the police station to court and prison. It includes a record of the examination of your client by the police surgeon, psychiatrist, ASW or CPN. This should alert the gaolers to any suicide or self-harm risk and they should make frequent checks on your client in the cells. If there is a mental health assessment scheme at the court, he may have been referred to the scheme by the gaolers. If not you should make the referral. In the absence of a court scheme, you can ask that a police surgeon be called to examine your client.

7.8.2 Your client may say that a remand in custody will make him harm himself. A bail application based on this assertion may well be refused on the basis that he should be in custody for his own protection, unless a suitable alternative package can be set up, or a remand to hospital is possible. If your client's application for bail fails and no hospital bed is available, you should ask the court to endorse on the warrant to the prison any concerns about the client's state of mind. A similar note must be made on the Prisoner Escort Record (PER) which accompanies the prisoner. After the hearing, it can be helpful to try and discuss your concerns about your client with the Prison Medical Officer so as to obtain appropriate care for him in custody. Your client may be transferred from prison to hospital for medical treatment under s.48 of the Act.

Protection of others

7.8.3 You may be placed in a difficult position if your client makes clear and apparently serious threats against other people. Generally the duty of confidentiality is paramount, although in extreme circumstances it may be over-ruled (see paras. 3.5.8.–3.5.11 for guidance).

7.8.4 More frequently, your client's behaviour may be intimidating to a point where you are concerned for your own safety. This is a particular problem for a duty solicitor when you and the client have no previous knowledge of each other. Gaolers often give warnings about how dangerous a defendant is, most of which turn out to be well-intentioned but unnecessary. Like most clients, mentally disordered defendants will recognise that you are on their side, once you have introduced yourself and explained your role. However, some may incorporate you into a system of paranoid beliefs produced by mental illness, in which case there is no point in arguing with them. If you are worried it is unwise to be locked into a cell or interview room with the client, unless there is a gaoler within eyesight or earshot.

7.9 Taking instructions

7.9.1 Despite your client's mental state, you must as far as possible take the instructions and other details outlined in paras. 7.2.2–7.2.4, drawing on whatever sources of information are available. If your client was assisted in the police station by an appropriate adult or ASW whom you can contact, this may be a useful source of information as they may have made enquiries about his circumstances. It is essential that your client understands court procedure especially if this is his first appearance at court. The booklet, *You're on Trial*, published in the series Books Beyond Words, will help clients with learning difficulties to understand court procedures.

7.9.2 You may often be unable to obtain instructions at the first appearance, when your client is distressed and unwell. He may say that he does not wish to be represented, in which case you must explain this to the court. The court can grant you legal aid anyway, in the hope that he changes his mind. It is important to note that rapid improvement may occur once he has some treatment and is out of the court and police station setting. For this reason you should make arrangements to see your client as soon as possible after the court hearing.

7.10 Fitness to plead

7.10.1 If your client is mute or otherwise incapable of giving you instructions, because of severe mental impairment, or due to persistent delusions which affect his understanding of the trial, he may be deemed 'unfit to plead'. You should always instruct the psychiatrist who is examining your client to address this point specifically. The test of fitness to plead is an old common law test deriving from the case of *Pritchard* (1836) 7 C&P 303. The doctor must assess whether the defendant is able to exercise his right to challenge jurors, understand details of the evidence and give evidence himself at trial, and instruct his legal advisers.

7.10.2 In most instances, if your client is unfit to plead, he is also likely to be suffering from a mental disorder within the terms of s.1, Mental Health Act 1983. The magistrates' court is likely to proceed by way of a hospital order under s.37. The provisions of s.37 (3) (see para. 7.13.3) may be used when your client is unable to enter a plea to the charge against him. The court has no power to proceed in this way if the charge is triable on indictment only, or if it is non-imprisonable. Some clients, for example those whose mental state cannot be assessed since they are persistently mute, may be deemed unfit to plead although it cannot be safely said that they are suffering from a mental disorder within the terms of the Act.

7.10.3 In rare cases, when your client is charged with an offence triable on indictment and a hospital order is not a possibility, the issue of unfitness must be dealt with at the Crown court under the procedure set out in the Criminal Procedure (Insanity and Unfitness to Plead) Act 1991. If medical evidence of unfitness is presented by either the defence or the prosecution, it is for a jury to decide, on the basis of that evidence, whether the defendant will be able to comprehend the course of the proceedings so as to make a proper defence. There is no similar power granted to magistrates to make a finding of unfitness, so if your client is charged with a summary-only offence, there may be a trial on the basis of an insanity defence, which is outside the scope of this book.

7.11 Mental health assessment schemes

7.11.1 Concern at the numbers of mentally disordered offenders remanded in custody for long periods while awaiting medical reports has led to the establishment of court mental health assessment schemes, usually run by local mental health services. The schemes vary widely from court to court. Some are staffed by an ASW and two doctors, some by a single doctor, and others consist solely of a CPN or psychiatric social worker. You should acquaint yourself with your local schemes so that you are aware where and when they operate, the staff involved and the particular arrangements in place. The immediate assistance they can offer depends on the level of staffing because, for example, to detain someone under s.3 of the Act, an ASW is needed to make the application, with the written opinions of two doctors in support, whereas a remand to hospital under s.35 can be effected by the report of a single doctor. However, CPN-led schemes can work well where there is an agreed means of calling in a doctor and ASW when needed.

7.11.2 If your client is examined by the staff available on the court scheme, you will be able to get an immediate assessment as to whether a mental health disposal of the case is feasible, even if a further remand will be necessary. All can offer invaluable advice about the client's mental state, the local options available and the mechanics of effecting his admission to hospital. Most schemes deal principally with defendants likely to be remanded into custody without immediate psychiatric intervention.

7.11.3 If your client has no ties to the mental health services but is willing to be examined by a member of the mental health assessment scheme which operates at court on a different day, you may ask the court to remand him to that day. If a court does not have such scheme the case may be remitted to another local court which has one. This may well be easier and quicker than obtaining an appointment with the relevant catchment area psychiatrist, unless you are confident in your knowledge of local services. It also has the advantage that you do not need to apply to the Legal Aid Board for prior authority to pay for a report. It may also be advisable if, for example, your client's bail address is temporary or if for any other reason the delay involved in arranging an outpatient's appointment would be detrimental to the client's interests.

7.11.4 Your client may insist that he is well and has no need to see a doctor. Even if you disagree, you should not press him to do so. Your client's behaviour may well make his mental health problems obvious to the court, in which case the court is likely to order a report on your client whether or not he wishes it. You must advise him that the court has the power to order reports notwithstanding his objections and although he does not have to speak to the doctor, it may be in his best interests to do so.

7.12 Reports

7.12.1 The court has various powers to order medical reports both before and after plea and to ensure the defendant's co-operation with their preparation. These are in addition to the power to ensure the defendant's co-operation with reports under s.3 (6), Bail Act 1976, mentioned above at para. 7.7.2.

7.12.2 The responsibility for payment to doctors for reports varies from court to court but generally reports ordered by the court to be obtained by the Probation Service are paid for by them; reports from prison are supplied without charge by the prison Health Care Service and reports provided by the defence must be paid for by solicitors, with prior authority from the LAB. It is important to clarify on each occasion which agency is responsible for requesting and paying for the reports.

7.12.3 Under s.54 of the Mental Health Act 1983 a copy of any medical report prepared for the court must be given to the defendant's solicitor if he is represented. If the defendant is not represented the contents of the report must be explained to him. Either the court or the defendant may request the author of the report to attend to give oral evidence, and the defendant may call evidence to rebut the contents of the report.

7.12.4 If your client is remanded into custody for the preparation of reports, it is advisable to supply the prison psychiatrist with detailed information about his history and background, particularly if there has been recent inpatient treatment as this may encourage a fuller and more helpful report.

7.12.5 Most prison Health Care Centres are visited weekly by a local catchment area psychiatrist, generally with forensic experience and it may well be helpful to contact that doctor to discuss your client's case. You may be able to persuade the prison doctor to recommend to the Home Secretary that he transfer your client to hospital under s.48 of the Act if he is in urgent need of treatment. (The full text of s.48 is set out in Appendix 2.) Written reports from two doctors are needed to make the recommendation. A transfer direction made under s.48 automatically places your client on a restriction direction throughout the period of transfer.

7.12.6 Prison Health Care Centres are not necessarily staffed by trained psychiatrists and do not constitute a 'hospital' within the terms of the Act. Thus no treatment without consent is possible except for common law emergency powers to treat. This can mean that floridly psychotic clients go untreated. It is acknowledged that a prison setting is the least appropriate option for care of a mentally disordered offender (see Home Office Circular 66/90, para. 7 at Appendix 5).

Section 30 of the Magistrates' Court Act 1980: reports for sentencing

7.12.7 This section provides that where on the trial of an offence punishable on summary conviction with imprisonment, if the court is satisfied that the accused did the act/made the omission charged but is of the opinion that a medical report on his physical or mental condition (or both) is necessary before disposing of the case, it may require a report. Note that the court need not proceed to conviction of your client if it is satisfied that he did the act/ made the omission charged. This is comparable to the power to make a hospital order without conviction set out in s.37 (3), the Act (see below, para. 7.13.3).

7.12.8 Remand periods for reports under s.30 are three weeks at a time if in custody, and four weeks if on bail. If your client is on bail the court must impose a condition requiring him to co-operate with the preparation of the report. Rule 24 of the Magistrates' Court Rules 1981 states that, when exercising its right to request a report under s.30, the court must send to the doctor at the prison or other place where the defendant is to be examined, a statement of the reasons for the request and any information before the court about the defendant's physical or mental condition. Such reports are generally obtained by the Probation Service (and at their expense). It is worthwhile liaising with them to ensure that any background information your client wishes disclosed is supplied to them.

Section 35 of the Mental Health Act: reports in hospital

7.12.9 This provision allows the defendant to be remanded to a hospital for the preparation of reports. The full text of this section is set out in Appendix 2. The single report necessary to effect the remand to hospital for a fuller assessment can be provided by the court duty psychiatrist if suitably qualified. It is important to note that this power may be used prior to any indication of plea if the defendant consents. If you consider that the court is unlikely to permit your client to be remanded on bail for the preparation of reports, you may wish to advise your client to consent to the use of s.35.

7.12.10 Remand to hospital under s.35 has the advantage to your client of ensuring that he receives care in hospital, undoubtedly clinically preferable to a prison setting. The court may be reluctant to make the order, as the section contains no stipulation that the defendant will be held on a locked ward. The court may think that the hospital wing of a remand prison protects the public more effectively, unless given assurances of secure conditions by the admitting doctor. A hospital may be reluctant to admit a highly disturbed defendant under s.35 as the Act provides no power under this section to medicate or treat the patient without consent, save for common law emergency powers.

7.12.11 Paragraph 17.3 of the Mental Health Act Code of Practice recommends that when a patient remanded under s.35 is thought to be in need of medical treatment for a mental disorder under Part IV of the Act, i.e. medical treatment under ss.2–3 of the Act, the patient should be referred back to court as soon as possible with the appropriate medical recommendations (for a hospital order under s.37), or, failing that, consideration should be given to whether the patient meets the criteria for detention under ss.2 or 3 of the Act. Detention under these sections will give the hospital the power of treatment (or assessment followed by treatment). The report by Christopher Clunis into the murder of Jonathan Zito states that if a patient remanded to hospital by a court fits the admission criteria for a civil section, he should be so sectioned to avoid his precipitate discharge from hospital if the criminal proceedings are abandoned for any reason.

7.12.12 If your client is willing to enter hospital by this method and the admitting doctor detains him under s.3, the task of persuading the CPS that the public interest will not be served by continuing to prosecute him will be made considerably easier. There is little difference in practice between the civil treatment section and the hospital order under s.37 of the Act save that the patient detained under s.37 may not apply to a Mental Health Review Tribunal until after six months have elapsed.

7.13 Disposals available to the court

7.13.1 The court may deal with the mentally disordered offender in any of the usual ways, i.e. conditional discharge, fine, probation, community service or combination order, although in each case they must take into account the offender's ability to comply with the terms of the sentence. Specific disposals appropriate to mentally disordered offenders include hospital orders under s.37 of the Act, probation orders with a condition of treatment and committal for sentence to the Crown court for the imposition of a restriction order under ss.37–41 of the Act.

Section 37 of the Mental Health Act 1983: hospital order

7.13.2 (a) This is an order for compulsory hospital treatment for a minimum of six months, which is the principal means available to the magistrates' court to ensure that a mentally disordered offender receives treatment rather than punishment. The section is set out in full in Appendix 2 and contains essential procedural requirements as to reports and the necessity of a hospital bed being available. There is no power for the magistrates to make such an order in respect of a non-imprisonable offence. Advice to the CPS is that where a hospital order appears to be appropriate, care should be taken not to reduce the offence to a non-imprisonable one, for example s.5, Public Order Act 1986. There is no stipulation in the section that there must be a causative link between the offence and your client's mental disorder.

(b) The court may make a hospital order without the defendant's consent. If your client objects there is little that you can do to prevent the making of the order unless you find a doctor who is prepared to give evidence in rebuttal. In such a case, which will be rare, you would wish the court to hear oral evidence. If your client will agree to outpatient treatment as a condition of a probation order, that proposal can be put to the court as an alternative to the hospital order, again with the support of medical evidence.

Hospital orders without conviction: s.37 (3), Mental Health Act 1983

7.13.3 (a) This provision, set out in full in Appendix 2, applies only to those people suffering from mental illness or severe mental impairment as defined by s.1. of the Act. The procedure for s.37 (3) is that the court must have the two relevant reports and the hospital bed available as required for a s.37 hospital order before the court can proceed to make the finding that the defendant has committed the act or made the omission charged. The section cannot be used to commit a defendant to the Crown court for the making of a restriction order.

(b) In practice, the section is a shortcut procedure which allows a hospital order to be made with the least possible delay once medical opinion supports it. It can be used to prevent difficult trials involving a mentally disordered offender and perhaps the victim of a crime committed by him wherever possible. In some courts even if a defendant is thought to be unfit to plead, the s.37 (3) procedure is followed if the other criteria for admission under the Act are satisfied. While different courts may adopt different procedures, normal practice is that the crucial prosecution evidence as to *actus reus* is read to the court if accepted by the defence in s.9 CJA form. If not accepted by way of s.9, the victim or other vital witness will be called to give evidence (which may require an adjournment). It appears that the court need not satisfy itself as to the issue of *mens rea*.

(c) If a legally represented defendant is too confused to consent to summary trial, it appears that the finding can be made in any event (see *R.* v. *Lincolnshire, Kesteven Justices ex p. O'Connor* [1983] 1 WLR 335, DC). The Divisional Court has found that even in cases where the defendant has elected trial on an offence triable either way, the court may make an order under this section if satisfied that the act/omission took place. See *R.* v. *Ramsgate Justices, ex p. Kazmarek* (1985) 80 Cr App R 366. The magistrates' court may not, however, make a hospital order on an offence triable only on indictment (*R.* v. *Chippenham Magistrates' Court, ex p. Thompson* (1995) The Times, 16 December). The nature of the finding is a matter of debate and although the section states that the court are not 'convicting' the defendant, the order will appear on the defendant's list of criminal convictions and will act on the mind of any future court considering sentence.

Section 41 of the Mental Health Act 1983: restriction order

7.13.4 Magistrates have no power to make a restriction order, but it may be suggested to them in medical reports that the nature of the offence, the defendant's antecedents, and the risk of his committing further offences if set at large, make one likely or appropriate in a particular case. If so, they must commit the defendant in custody to the Crown court for sentence. The power to commit for sentence is contained in s.43 of the Act.

Probation with a condition of medical treatment (Powers of Criminal Courts Act 1973, Sched. 1A, para. 5 as amended)

7.13.5 (a) A probation order may be made after a conviction of the defendant (not under the procedure in s.37 (3) of the Act). The order is subject to the usual requirements of a community penalty. A condition for treatment can only be attached to the order if the court receives a written or oral report from an approved mental health specialist that the defendant would benefit from such treatment but his condition is not such as to merit a hospital order. The treatment must be outlined in the order and can include outpatient treatment by a named medical practitioner, or outpatient or (unusually) inpatient treatment at a named mental health facility. The 'medical practitioner' may be a chartered psychologist. The court cannot attach the condition to a probation order unless satisfied that arrangements have been made for the provision of the treatment outlined in the condition.

(b) The defendant must consent to the proposed arrangements for treatment. If he does not, the probation order cannot be made. A similar requirement to undergo treatment can be attached to a supervision order imposed by the Youth court. A young person aged over 14 years must consent to the terms of the treatment imposed by the condition.

(c) Probation may be a suitable disposal when your client does not require inpatient care or has been treated in hospital since the commission of the offence so that his mental state has improved to a point where care in the community is appropriate. The order requires the client to keep appointments and accept treatment, although it cannot require him to take prescribed medication. It is usually not suitable for a person who is not actively compliant with treatment or one with a very chaotic lifestyle.

Imprisonment

7.13.6 (a) By virtue of s.4, Criminal Justice Act 1991, the court must obtain and consider a medical report on any defendant who is, or appears to be, mentally disordered before imposing a custodial sentence. However, such a report may be dispensed with if the court considers that it is not necessary. Section 4(3) further provides that before passing a sentence of imprisonment (other than one fixed by law) on an offender who is or appears to be mentally disordered the court shall consider:

(i) any information before it which relates to his mental condition (whether given in a medical report, pre-sentence report or otherwise); and

(ii) the likely effect of such a sentence on that condition and on any treatment which may be available for it.

(b) The Home Office recognises that prison is likely to have a detrimental effect on the mental health of a mentally disordered offender. Home Office Circular 66/90 Provision for Mentally Disordered Offenders states:

'It is the Government's policy to divert mentally disordered persons from the criminal justice system in cases where the public interest does not require their prosecution. Where prosecution is necessary, it is important to find non-penal disposals wherever appropriate and the police courts and probation services are asked to work together with their local health and

social services to make effective use of the provisions of the Mental Health Act 1983 and the services which exist to help the mentally disordered offender.'

(c) Such a statement of intent, coupled with the requirements for reports, ought to mean that even where prosecution of mentally disordered persons is considered necessary, a sentence of imprisonment is unusual, especially for the less serious offences dealt with by the magistrates' court.

(d) However, where a hospital order is not recommended and yet the nature of the offence or the accused's criminal record suggests that protection of the public is required, the advocate must be very aware that prison is an option. There is also a possibility of extended sentences being imposed under s.2 (2)(b), Criminal Justice Act 1991, a power rarely used by magistrates themselves but which may persuade them to commit a mentally disordered offender for sentence. Such an approach may be adopted when a client suffers from a personality disorder which is 'untreatable' (and therefore not within the ambit of the Act) and yet he is likely to cause further harm to the public if not detained. Offenders suffering from a psychopathic disorder may be made subject to a hospital and limitation direction under s.45A of the Act, as inserted by s.46 of the Crime Sentences Act 1997, by a Crown court only. (See Appendix 2 for the full text of this section.)

Appendices

Sources of law and guidance

The following publications contain the law, government policy and directives concerning mentally disordered offenders.

Mental Health Act 1983

Contains the law relating to the detention and treatment of mentally disordered persons. The most useful edition, with invaluable notes, is Richard Jones' *Mental Health Act Manual* 6th edn (London: Sweet & Maxwell 1999), which also contains the Code of Practice to the Act and the Mental Health Review Tribunal Rules.

Code of Practice to Mental Health Act 1983

Chapter 3 of the Code contains new and important material about patients concerned with criminal proceedings. Paragraphs 3.7–3.14 which give guidance to doctors preparing reports on such patients are reproduced at Appendix 6 (Department of Health and Welsh Office 1999).

Mental Health (Patients in the Community) Act 1995

Inserts into the Mental Health Act 1983 the 'supervised discharge' provisions (s. 25, MHA).

Memorandum on the Mental Health Act (1998 edition)

Contains government guidance on the main provisions of the MHA and acts a clear and useful summary. (The Stationery Office).

Homicide Act 1957

Contains the provisions of the defence of diminished responsibility to a charge of murder, by reason of 'mental abnormality'.

Criminal Procedure (Insanity and Unfitness to Plead) Act 1991

Contains the provisions of the Crown Court 'unfitness to plead' procedure and the defence of insanity.

Criminal Justice Act 1991

Contains, *inter alia*, the power under s.2 for a court sentencing a violent or sexual

ADVISING MENTALLY DISORDERED OFFENDERS

offender to impose an 'extended sentence'. This is of particular relevance to offenders who suffer from an untreatable personality disorder.

Criminal Justice Act 1998

See in particular ss. 58–60 which provide for extended post-release supervision of sexual offenders, for a period of up to 10 years, including those who have served an extended sentence.

Crime Sentences Act 1997

Section 46 deals with the Crown court power to make hospital and limitation directions on psychopathic offenders. Section 47 contains the Crown court power to direct the admission for treatment of a mentally disordered offender to a named unit of a hospital.

Prosecution of Offences Act 1985

Contains the power of the CPS to discontinue proceedings.

Code of Practice for Crown Prosecutors

Contains guidance on the principles which should govern the CPS in deciding whether charges against mentally disordered persons should be discontinued.

Police and Criminal Evidence Act 1984 and Codes of Practice

Legal Aid Board Duty Solicitor Arrangements 1999 (Legal Aid Board)

The Law Society's Guidelines for Legal Representatives at Mental Health Tribunals 1998

Issued in May 1998, they are helpful with regard to ethical questions faced when representing the mentally disordered client (The Law Society.)

Home Office Circulars

Concerning mentally disordered offenders: Numbers 59/90, 66/90, 93/91, 12/95 and 52/97 (Home Office.)

Mentally Disordered Offenders: Inter-Agency Working 1995

A booklet on best practice issued with Home Office Circular 12/95.

Definitions: medical and legal

MEDICAL DEFINITIONS

Acute

A severe or sharp period of illness, often short-lived.

Affect

Mood or emotional state, as in 'flat' affect. Affective disorders are those with persisting abnormal mood. Flattening of affect is also observed as a symptom of schizophrenia.

Approved social worker (ASW)

Under s. 114, Mental Health Act 1983 a local authority must appoint a sufficient number of ASWs to discharge the functions conferred on them under the Act. To be approved, a social worker has to undertake special training in working with clients with mental disorders and the law relating to their treatment and detention under the Mental Health Act 1983. An ASW makes the application, supported by medical opinion(s), which leads to detention in hospital under ss. 2–4 of the Act. The ASW must consult or inform the 'nearest relative' of the patient and arrange the patient's transfer to hospital.

Bipolar

Describes morbid mood fluctuations between two extremes, for example the high and low moods associated with manic depression.

Bis die (BD)

Twice a day, in the administration of medication.

Catatonia

A state of stupor or immobility, often with strange bodily postures, which may be marked by sudden and violent changes from one state to another.

Catchment area

Geographical division of a community allocated to a Hospital Trust responsible for mental health care. Within each area, sectors usually have a consultant psychiatrist (catchment area RMO) presiding over a specialist team of CPNs, ASWs, etc., responsible for providing care in the community as well as for inpatient admission to a local psychiatric ward.

Chronic

Of an illness, long-standing (though not necessarily severe).

Community psychiatric nurse (CPN)

A registered mental nurse working in the community, often attached to a CRMO's team, who visits clients at home to administer medication and assess their mental health. This can be part of a care programme under the Care Programme Approach (CPA).

DSM IV

Diagnostic and Statistical Manual of Mental Disorders, Fourth revision (American Psychiatric Association, 1994). The system of classification and description of mental disorders employed by the American Psychiatric Association. Used in parallel with ICD 10.

Forensic

A forensic psychiatrist and other members of the multi-disciplinary team (e.g. social workers) deal with the interface between law and psychiatry. In practice, most of their clinical work relates to mentally disordered offenders.

Guardian

Person appointed under s.7 MHA 1983, normally a social worker but may be another person approved by the local social services, who acquires certain powers in relation to a patient in the community. These powers include directing where the person shall live, ensuring that he receives visits from medical and social service professionals, and that he attends at a specified day centre or other places for treatment. These powers are infrequently used, but tend to be used mainly in the case of patients suffering from mental impairment. Compare and contrast with Supervised Discharge under s. 25 MHA 1983.

Hospital managers

Each NHS hospital Trust must appoint committees of lay persons to exercise specific legal duties on the Trust's behalf including ensuring that the power to detain patients under the Mental Health Act 1983 is properly exercised and the documentation requirements are complied with, review the need for the patient's continuing detention as well as any application by the RMO to renew the section.

ICD 10

International Classification of Mental and Behavioural Disorders, 10th revision. Clinical descriptions and diagnostic guidelines (World Health Organization, 1992). Sets out the internationally accepted descriptive criteria for identifying mental disorders.

IM

Medication given intramuscularly by injection.

Key nurse

Mental health nurse with primary responsibility for the patient's care while on a hospital ward as an inpatient. Sometimes referred to as a primary nurse.

Key worker

Worker (who may be a social worker or a mental health nurse) who has particular responsibility for a client's care while either attending a centre or as a resident of a mental health hostel.

Nearest relative

The closest relative to the patient as defined in the list set out in s.26, MHA 1983. This person has important rights in relation to the patient, both before admission (the right to request an ASW to assess the patient's mental state and in some cases to make an application for their admission to hospital), and after admission (the right to discharge the patient detained under ss.2 or 3 from hospital in some circumstances). The ASW must consult and inform the nearest relative of a proposed application to admit a patient.

PRN

Pro re nata; of medication, prescribed to be used not regularly, but only when required, for example to control extreme agitation.

Reactive

As in reactive depression; episode of illness which arises as a response to adverse circumstances, for example, bereavement.

93

Responsible medical officer (RMO)

The registered medical practitioner, normally a consultant psychiatrist, responsible for the patient's care in hospital, or, in the community, in which case he is known as the Community RMO (CRMO). Each RMO will normally have a geographical catchment area of responsibility or a psychiatric specialism, e.g. forensic psychiatry, mental impairment.

Section 12 doctor

Registered medical practitioner approved by the Health Authority under guidelines laid down by the Secretary of State under the provisions of s.12, Mental Health Act 1983, i.e. with specialist psychiatric training.

Ter die sumendus (TDS)

Three times a day.

LEGAL DEFINITIONS

Mental Health Act 1983: summary of main holding and detention powers under the Act.

Civil sections

Section 2 Admission for assessment

Authorises the compulsory admission to hospital for assessment (or assessment followed by treatment) for up to 28 days of a patient who:

(a) is suffering from mental disorder of a nature or degree which warrants the detention of the patient in hospital for assessment (for assessment followed by treatment) for at least a limited period; and

(b) ought to be so detained in the interests of his own health and safety or for the protection of others.

The application must be made by an ASW or the patient's nearest relative and must be supported by the medical recommendations of two doctors, both of whom must have seen and examined the patient in the five days preceding the making of the recommendation and one of whom must be approved as having special experience in the diagnosis or treatment of mental disorder. The patient has a right to apply to an MHRT for discharge.

Section 3 Admission for treatment

Authorises the compulsory admission and detention in hospital for treatment for a period of up to six months of a patient who is suffering from one of the four forms of mental disorder set out in s. 1 of the Act. The mental disorder must be of a nature or degree which makes it appropriate for the patient to receive medical treatment in a hospital and it must be necessary for the health and safety of the patient or for the protection of others that he should receive such treatment. It cannot be provided unless he is detained under this section. In the case of patients suffering from psychopathic disorder or mental impairment it must be likely that the medical treatment is likely to alleviate or prevent a deterioration in the patient's condition. The application may be made by the nearest relative or by an ASW who must have consulted the nearest relative before the making of the application, unless this would cause unreasonable delay or is not reasonably practicable. The application cannot be made if the nearest relative objects but if these objections are unreasonable, the ASW may make an application to the County court to displace the nearest relative. The application must be supported by two medical recommendations as laid out in relation to s. 2 above. The patient has a right to apply to an MHRT.

Sections 4 and 5 Emergency provisions

Section 4 — the ASW or nearest relative may make an application for an emergency admission for assessment of the patient for up to 72 hours, on the basis that it is of 'urgent necessity' for the patient to be admitted for assessment and compliance with the provisions of s. 2 would involve undesirable delay. The application is supported by one written medical recommendation, stating that the patient is suffering from a mental disorder and verifying the statement made in the application.

Section 5 — contains the authority for emergency holding of a person who is already a patient while measures are taken to assess him with a view to further detention under ss.2–3.

Section 5 (2) — permits the doctor in charge of the treatment of an informal patient to detain him for up to 72 hours if the doctor believes that an application under ss.2 or 3 ought to be made.

Section 5 (4) — permits a qualified mental nurse to detain for up to six hours a patient who is already being treated for mental disorder if it appears to him that:

(a) the patient is suffering from mental disorder to such a degree that it is necessary for his health or safety or for the protection of others for him to be immediately restrained from leaving the hospital; and

(b) it is not practicable to secure the immediate attendance of a doctor to furnish a report under s.5(2).

Both powers to hold the patient come into force once the relevant medical opinion has been recorded in writing on the prescribed form and in the case of s.5(2), that opinion has been delivered to Hospital Managers or their authorised officer (usually the Mental Health Act Administrator).

Sections 7 and 8 Guardianship

A mentally disordered person (not necessarily an inpatient) may be subject to a guardianship order made under s.7. The powers of the guardian are set out in s.8. The grounds for guardianship are that the patient is suffering from one of the four forms of mental disorder and that guardianship is necessary in the interests of the patient's welfare or for the protection of other persons. The procedure for the application and medical recommendations is similar to that for an admission for treatment under s.3. The guardian may:

(a) require the patient to live at an address specified by the guardian;

(b) require the patient to attend specified places at specified times for medical treatment, education, occupation or training; and

(c) require access to the patient to be given at the place where the patient is living to any doctor, ASW or other person specified by the guardian.

The guardian appointed is normally a social worker although it may be a person approved by social services, such as a relative of the patient. The patient has a right to apply to an MHRT.

Section 25 Aftercare under supervision

Contains the provisions for aftercare under supervision, or 'supervised discharge', whereby a patient discharged from hospital after treatment under s.3 may be required:

(a) to live at a particular place;

(b) should attend a particular place at set times for medical treatment, education, occupation and training, and

(c) should permit access to his doctor, ASW, supervisor or person authorised by the supervisor at his place of residence.

The Act gives the supervisor power to take and convey the patient to his place of residence or to any place designated under the terms of the order for treatment, education etc., but does not give the power to medicate the patient against his wishes.

The grounds for the order are (a) that the patient is suffering from one of the four forms of mental disorder defined under the Act; (b) that there would be substantial risk of serious harm to the health or safety of the patient or to the safety of others, or of the patient being seriously exploited if the patient did not receive aftercare services under s.117 of the Act, and (c) that supervision is likely to ensure that the patient receives those services. The application procedure is complex and

96

lengthy and has meant that this provision, and that of guardianship, is little used in practice. The patient has a right to apply to an MHRT.

Criminal proceedings

Section 35 Remand for reports

Power of magistrates' and Crown courts to remand an accused to hospital for the preparation of a report on his mental condition. The power may be exercised by the magistrates' court in relation to a person who has been convicted of an offence punishable on summary conviction with imprisonment, or one who is charged with such an offence and the court is satisfied that he did the act or made the omission charged or he has consented to the exercise of the power. The court must be satisfied on the written evidence of one s.12 approved registered medical practitioner that there is reason to believe that the accused is suffering from one of the four forms of mental disorder defined in s.1 of the Act; and that it would be impracticable for a report to be prepared if he were on bail; and, based on written or oral evidence of a doctor or other representative of the admitting hospital, that a bed will be available for the accused within seven days. The same power on the same evidence, may be exercised by the Crown court in relation to any person awaiting trial at the Crown court or post conviction (save in the case of a person convicted of murder). Remand in the first instance is for 28 days, and may be extended for further 28-day periods, up to a maximum of 12 weeks, if the court has evidence from the doctor responsible for preparing the report that such further remands are necessary for completing the assessment.

Section 36 Remand for treatment

Power of the Crown court to direct the remand to hospital for treatment of an accused person who is awaiting trial at any stage of the proceedings and who is charged with an offence punishable with imprisonment other than murder.

Section 37 Hospital order

Where a person is convicted of an offence punishable on summary conviction with imprisonment and the court is satisfied on the written or oral evidence of two registered medical practitioners that the accused is suffering from a mental disorder (as defined in s.1 MHA) of a nature or degree which makes it appropriate for him to be detained in a hospital for medical treatment (and in the case of psychopathic disorder or mental impairment that such treatment is likely to alleviate or to prevent a deterioration in his condition) and the court is of opinion that having regard to all the circumstances including the nature of the offence and the character and antecedents of the offender and to the other available methods of dealing with him, that an order under this section would be the most suitable method of disposing of the case, the court shall authorise the admission to, and detention in, such hospital as is specified in the order. The order is for six months with no right to apply to an MHRT until after renewal which may be for another six months and then yearly.

Section 37 (3) Hospital order without conviction

The section provides that where a person is charged before a magistrates' court with any act or omission as an offence and the court would have power on convicting him of the offence to make a hospital order, then if the court is satisfied that the accused did the act or made the omission charged, it may if it thinks fit, make the order without convicting him.

Section 38 Interim hospital order

The power of the magistrates' court to authorise the admission and detention of a convicted offender to a hospital for treatment for a trial period to allow the courts and the hospital to assess the offender's response to treatment and the suitability of a hospital order as a means of disposing of the case. Initially for a period of up to 12 weeks, the order can be renewed to a total maximum period of 12 months before sentence takes place. The Crown court may make such an order in respect of a convicted or an unconvicted person.

Section 41 Restriction order

The Crown court alone may make a restriction order in addition to a hospital order if it appears to the court that, having regard to (a) the nature of the offence, and (b) the antecedents of the offender and (c) the risk of his committing further offences if discharged, that a restriction order is necessary for the protection of the public from serious harm, and that at least one of the registered medical practitioners whose evidence is taken into account has given oral evidence to the court. If a magistrates' court is satisfied that the conditions exist which would permit it to make a hospital order but consider that a restriction order should also be made, it may commit the offender (over 14 years old) to the Crown court under s.43, MHA.

Section 45A MHA (inserted by s.46 Crime (Sentences) Act 1997) hospital and limitation direction

In relation to offenders suffering from psychopathic disorder the Crown court has power, when imposing a prison sentence on offenders for any offence other than murder, to make a 'hospital and limitation direction' to direct their immediate detention in a specified hospital (a 'hospital direction'), together with an order that they be subject to the restrictions of s.41 (a 'limitation direction'). Such an order may be made on the evidence of two doctors that:

(i) the offender is suffering from a psychopathic disorder (together with any other mental disorder);

(ii) the (psychopathic) disorder is of a nature or degree which makes it appropriate for him to be detained in hospital for medical treatment;

(iii) such treatment is likely to alleviate or prevent a deterioration in his condition.

The effect of such an order is that from the start of the prison sentence the offender will be managed in hospital as if subject to a restriction order. However, if the RMO considers that no further treatment is likely to be beneficial, he may transfer the offender back to prison to serve the remainder of his sentence.

Sections 47 and 48 Transfer of prisoners to hospital

Under s.48 the Home Secretary may make a direction that any person remanded in custody by a magistrates' court should be transferred to hospital. He must, when making such a direction in respect of a prisoner, also make a 'restriction direction' (under s.49), which confers on the patient the same status as a patient under s.41. The Home Secretary must be satisfied on the evidence of two written reports from two registered medical practitioners, one of whom must be approved under s.12, that:

(i) the prisoner is suffering from mental illness or severe mental impairment; and

(ii) the mental illness or severe mental impairment is of a nature or degree which makes it appropriate for the prisoner to be detained in hospital for medical treatment; and

(iii) the prisoner is in urgent need of such treatment.

Section 47 gives the Home Secretary a similar power to transfer convicted prisoners serving a sentence of imprisonment to hospital for treatment subject to various requirements as to medical reports similar to those in s.37.

Checklists

Listed below are a number of prompts to assist you in taking instructions from a mentally disordered or handicapped client at the police station. The points do not include all the general information you obtain when representing a client in a police station. You are referred to the checklists in *Defending Suspects at Police Stations*, Ed Cape (LAG 1999) which cover all the other questions you should ask.

1. Mental disorder

- Diagnosis, for example, schizophrenia, depression
- Length of illness
- Symptoms of illness
- Dates of previous admissions to psychiatric hospital
- Admissions as in or out-patient
- Detained voluntarily or on section
- Civil (s.2 or s.3) or criminal section (ss.37–41)
- Date of last discharge from hospital
- Name, address and telephone number of most recent hospital
- Treatment including name of current medication
- Care in the community, e.g. supported hostel, day centre
- Name/telephone numbers of (C)RMO, social worker, key nurse, CPN etc.
- GP – name, address and telephone number
- Name, address and telephone number of nearest relative
- Consent of client to talk to:
  - Medical professionals
  - Other professionals
  - Nearest relative

2. Mental handicap (learning disability)

- Form of disability
  - Particular difficulties e.g. limited language ability (expression and/or understanding), memory recall, description of events

- IQ score (if known)
- Reading or writing difficulties
- Name and address of any special school attended
- Education Act statement by local authority
- Name/telephone of (C)RMO, social worker, key worker, portage worker etc.
- Dates of previous admissions to psychiatric hospital
- Admissions as in or out-patient
- Detained voluntarily or on section
- Name and address of hospital
- Date of last discharge from hospital
- Civil (s.2 or s.3) or criminal section (ss.37–41)
- Name, address and telephone number of nearest relative
- Consent of client to talk to:
  - Medical professionals
  - Other professionals
  - Nearest relative

APPENDIX 4

Annex E of the PACE Codes of Practice

Annex E: Summary of Provisions Relating to Mentally Disordered and Mentally Handicapped People

1. If an officer has any suspicion, or is told in good faith, that a person of any age may be mentally disordered or mentally handicapped, or mentally incapable of understanding the significance of questions put to him or his replies, then that person shall be treated as mentally disordered or mentally handicapped for the purposes of this code. [See paragraph 1.4]

2. In the case of a person who is mentally disordered or mentally handicapped, 'the appropriate adult' means:

    (a) a relative, guardian or some other person responsible for his care or custody;

    (b) someone who has experience of dealing with mentally disordered or mentally handicapped people but is not a police officer or employed by the police; or

    (c) failing either of the above, some other responsible adult aged 18 or over who is not a police officer or employed by the police

    [See paragraph 1.7 (b)]

3. If the custody officer authorises the detention of a person who is mentally handicapped or appears to be suffering from a mental disorder he must as soon as practicable inform the appropriate adult of the grounds for the person's detention and his whereabouts, and ask the adult to come to the police station to see the person. If the appropriate adult is already at the police station when information is given as required in paragraphs 3.1 to 3.5 the information must be given to the detained person in the appropriate adult's presence. If the appropriate adult is not at the police station when the provisions of 3.1 to 3.5 are complied with then these provisions must be complied with again in the presence of the appropriate adult once that person arrives. [See paragraphs 3.9 and 3.11]

4. If the appropriate adult, having been informed of the right to legal advice, considers that legal advice should be taken, the provisions of section 6 of the code apply as if the mentally disordered or mentally handicapped person had requested access to legal advice. [See paragraph 3.13 and Note E2]

5. If a person brought to the police station appears to be suffering from mental disorder or is incoherent other than through drunkenness alone, or if a detained person subsequently appears to be mentally disordered, the custody officer must immediately call the police station or, in urgent cases, send the person to hospital or call the nearest available medical practitioner. It is not intended that these provisions should delay the transfer of a person to a place of safety under section 136 of the Mental Health Act 1983 where that is applicable. Where an assessment under that Act is to take place at the police station, the custody officer has discretion not to call the police surgeon so long as he believes that the assessment by a registered medical practitioner can be undertaken without due delay. [See paragraph 9.2]

6. It is imperative that a mentally disordered or mentally handicapped person who has been detained under section 136 of the Mental Health Act 1983 should be assessed as soon as possible. If that assessment is to take place at the police station, an approved social worker and a registered medical practitioner shall be called to the police station as soon as possible in order to interview and examine the person. Once the person has been interviewed and examined and suitable arrangements have been made for his treatment or care, he can no longer be detained under section 136. The person shall not be released until he has been seen by both the approved social worker and the registered medical practitioner. [See paragraph 3.10]

7. If a mentally disordered or mentally handicapped person is cautioned in the absence of the appropriate adult, the caution must be repeated in the appropriate adult's presence. [See paragraph 10.6]

8. A mentally disordered or mentally handicapped person must not be interviewed or asked to provide or sign a written statement in the absence of the appropriate adult unless the provisions of paragraph 11.1 or Annex C of this code apply. Questioning in these circumstances may not continue in the absence of the appropriate adult once sufficient information to avert the risk has been obtained. A record shall be made of the grounds for any decision to begin an interview in these circumstances. [See paragraphs 11.1 and 11.14 and Annex C]

9. Where the appropriate adult is present at an interview, he shall be informed that he is not expected to act simply as an observer; and also that the purposes of his presence are, first, to advise the person being interviewed and to observe whether or not the interview is being conducted properly and fairly, and, secondly, to facilitate communication with the person being interviewed. [See paragraph 11.16]

10. If the detention of a mentally disordered or mentally handicapped person is reviewed by a review officer or a superintendent, the appropriate adult must, if available at the time, be given an opportunity to make representations to the officer about the need for continuing detention. [See paragraphs 15.1 and 15.2]

11. If the custody officer charges a mentally disordered or mentally handicapped person with an offence or takes such other action as is appropriate when there is sufficient evidence for a prosecution this must be done in the presence of the appropriate adult. The written notice embodying any charge must be given to the appropriate adult. [See paragraphs 16.1 to 16.3]

12. An intimate or strip search of a mentally disordered or mentally handicapped person may take place only in the presence of the appropriate adult of the same sex, unless the person specifically requests the presence of a particular adult of the opposite sex. A strip search may take place in the absence of an appropriate adult only in cases of urgency where there is a risk of serious harm to the person detained or to others. [See Annex A, paragraphs 5 and 11(c)]

13. Particular care must be taken when deciding whether to use handcuffs to restrain a mentally disordered or mentally handicapped person in a locked cell. [See paragraph 8.2]

Notes for Guidance

E1   In the case of mentally disordered or mentally handicapped people, it may in certain circumstances be more satisfactory for all concerned if the appropriate adult is someone who has experience or training in their care rather than a relative lacking such qualifications. But if the person himself prefers a relative to a better qualified stranger or objects to a particular person as the appropriate adult, his wishes should if practicable be respected. [See Note 1E]

E2   The purpose of the provision at paragraph 3.13 is to protect the rights of a mentally disordered or mentally handicapped person who does not understand the significance of what is being said to him. If the person wishes to exercise the right to legal advice, the appropriate action should be taken and not delayed until the appropriate adult arrives. [See Note 3G] A mentally disordered or mentally handicapped person should always be given an opportunity, when an appropriate adult is called to the police station, to consult privately with a solicitor in the absence of the appropriate adult if he wishes to do so. [See Note 1EE]

E3   It is important to bear in mind that although mentally disordered or mentally handicapped are people often capable of providing reliable evidence, they may, without knowing or wishing to do so, be particularly prone in certain circumstances to provide information which is unreliable, misleading or incriminating. Special care should therefore always be exercised in questioning such a person, and the appropriate adult involved, if there is any doubt about a person's mental state or capacity. Because of the risk of unreliable evidence, it is important to obtain corroboration of any facts admitted whenever possible. [See Note 11B]

E4   Because of the risks referred to in Note E3, which the presence of the appropriate adult is intended to minimise, officers of superintendent rank or above should exercise their discretion to authorise the commencement of an interview in the adult's absence only in exceptional cases, where it is necessary to avert an immediate risk of serious harm. [See paragraph 11.1 and Annex C and Note C1]

Note: This text forms the entirety of Annex E of Code C in the *Police and Criminal Evidence Act 1984: Codes of Practice (s.60(1)(a) and s.66).* The Stationery Office, 1997.

Extracts from Home Office Circular 66/90

PROVISION FOR MENTALLY DISORDERED OFFENDERS

The purpose of this circular is to draw the attention of the courts and those whose services are responsible for dealing with mentally disordered persons who commit, or are suspected of committing, criminal offences to:

(a) the legal powers which exist; and

(b) the desirability of ensuring effective cooperation between agencies to ensure that the best use is made of resources and that mentally disordered persons are not prosecuted where this is not required by the public interest.

Police

4. The first point of contact between the criminal justice system and a mentally disordered person is often the police, who may be called to intervene in incidents involving a mentally disordered person. There are a range of powers which are available to the police, and it is important that they establish close working relationships with local health, probation, and social services to assist them in exercising their powers:

> (i) Section 135 of the Mental Health Act 1983 provides a constable with a power to remove to a place of safety a person found in a place to which the public have access and who appears to be suffering from mental disorder within the meaning of the Act and in immediate need of care or control if the constable thinks it is necessary to do so in the interests of that person or for the protection of others. The person may be detained for a maximum of 72 hours. The power in this section may be used in relation to persons who have not committed an offence, and to those who have (or are suspected of having) committed an offence, but where it is not considered necessary in the public interest to arrest that person for the offence. Agreement should be reached with local hospitals and local social services departments so that persons detained under section 136 are assessed by a psychiatrist and interviewed by an Approved Social Worker as soon as possible for the purpose of making any necessary arrangements for the person's treatment or care. It is desirable that, wherever possible, the place of safety in which the person might be detained should be a hospital and not a police station. Guidance on the use of section 136 is contained in Chapter 10 of the Department of Health Code of Practice on the implementation of the Mental Health Act 1983 (a copy is attached in Annex A);

(ii) section 135 of the 1983 Act empowers a justice of the peace – on information on oath laid by an Approved Social Worker – to issue a warrant authorising any constable to enter specified premises to remove to a place of safety – which should normally be a hospital – a person believed to be suffering from mental disorder who has been, or is being, ill-treated, neglected or not kept under proper control, or who is living alone and unable to care for himself.

The warrant will authorise the person's detention in a place of safety for a maximum of 72 hours. The initiative in seeking a warrant will normally rest with an Approved Social Worker. The warrant may apply to any premises within the justice's jurisdiction, including private property to which the police powers under section 136 do not extend;

(iii) where it is suspected that a mentally disordered person may have committed an offence, consideration should be given – in consultation with the Crown Prosecution Service, where appropriate – to whether any formal action by the police is necessary, particularly where it appears that prosecution is not required in the public interest in view of the nature of the offence. If the suspect is able to meet the requirements for a caution to be administered, he might be cautioned. If the criteria for a caution are not met, the police should consider whether any action need be taken against the suspect. In some cases the public interest might be met by diverting mentally disordered persons from the criminal justice system and finding alternatives to prosecution, such as admission to hospital under sections 2 or 3 or to guardianship under section 7 of the 1983 Act or informal support in the community by social service departments. The development of effective liaison with health and social services authorities will play an essential role in developing satisfactory arrangements to respond constructively in such cases;

(iv) the questioning of mentally disordered persons suspected of committing offences is subject to the Code of Practice for the Detention, Treatment and Questioning of Persons by Police Officers issued under section 66 of the Police and Criminal Evidence Act 1984. (Annex E of the Code summarises the provisions relating to mentally ill and mentally handicapped persons.)

Paragraph 9.2 requires the custody officer immediately to call a police surgeon if a person brought to a police station or already detained there appears to be suffering from a mental disorder. In urgent cases the person must be sent to hospital. These requirements apply even if the person makes no request for medical attention. In the case of mentally disordered persons, chief officers of police may find it helpful to arrange with their local health authorities for psychiatrists to fill the role of police surgeon. Chief officers will be aware that even with the protection afforded by the Police and Criminal Evidence Act 1984, some mentally disordered offenders may make confessions which are untrue, and therefore it is always advisable to seek other evidence which may support or reject the suspect's story;

(v) where it is decided that the public interest requires the prosecution of a mentally disordered person for an offence it should be borne in mind that he has the same right as other suspects to bail after charge. If his mental state or other factors, such as homelessness, give rise to difficulties in releasing him on bail, arrangements should be made with the health, probation, and social services to ensure that appropriate support can be provided, such as admission to hospital, where his mental condition warrants it, or to a hostel, if the managers agree. Police bail cannot, of course, be subject to conditions of residence or medical treatment, but satisfactory arrangements provide for these on a voluntary basis and may enable police to release the suspect on bail rather than detain him pending his appearance before the magistrate's court;

(vi) after a mentally disordered person has been charged, wherever possible arrangements should be made with the health, probation, and social services for his assessment with a view to ensuring that he receives any medical treatment that may be necessary, and that the Crown Prosecution Service and court can be advised of any particular bail conditions or, after conviction, disposal that may be appropriate to his circumstances. At Annex B to this circular is a note outlining court psychiatric assessment arrangements which have been established at certain central London and at Peterborough magistrates' courts to secure expert medical advice when required. Chief officers of police may wish to explore with their local chief probation officers and health authorities the possibility of setting up similar arrangements to ensure that suspects who are thought to be mentally disordered and in need of medical assessment should be seen by a psychiatrist as soon as possible.

Crown Prosecution Service

6. Where proceedings are instituted against a person by the police, the papers will be referred to the Crown Prosecution Service which will review the sufficiency of the evidence and consider carefully whether or not the public interest requires a prosecution in accordance with the Code for Crown Prosecutors. Any information provided by the police with the papers regarding that person's mental condition, or discussions held with other agencies to consider the advisability of diverting him from court, will be taken into account. It will be important to distinguish between those forms of mental disorder which are made worse by the institution of criminal proceedings and those forms of mental disorder which come about by reason of the institution of criminal proceedings. Where the Service is satisfied that the probable effect upon a person's mental health outweighs the interests of justice in the particular case, it will consider discontinuing the proceedings. Where the form of mental disorder is present without there being any indication that proceedings will have an adverse effect, the Crown Prosecutor will take account of the public interest in attempting to ensure that the offence will not be repeated as well as having regard to the welfare of the person in question.

MAGISTRATES' COURTS

7. Mentally disordered persons have the same rights as other persons, including a right to bail. A mentally disordered person should never be remanded to prison simply to receive medical treatment or assessment. It is desirable for the court to receive professional advice at as early a stage as possible on facilities which may be available to assist it with mentally disordered persons. Annex B to this circular describes court psychiatric assessments arrangements at certain central London and at Peterborough magistrates' courts. These enable the courts to receive speedy medical advice and to ensure that, where appropriate, arrangements can be made quickly to admit a mentally disordered person to hospital, for example as a condition of bail or, with the agreement of the hospital managers, under section 35 of the Mental Health Act 1983 following conviction. Where neither of these courses is applicable but the accused person nevertheless requires admission to hospital for assessment or treatment, the health and social services can be asked to consider using their civil powers of admission under sections 2 or 3 of the Act.

18. When a mentally disordered person is arrested and charged, the probation service should play its part in diverting him or her from custodial remand. They can do this in several ways. If there is a bail information scheme, the probation officer will visit the accused in police custody to interview him and obtain information which, if verified, can be passed on to the Crown Prosecution Service to inform the bail decision. Mentally disordered persons may be particularly at risk of being remanded in custody, because their circumstances and way of life may be unstable. Good liaison between the bail information scheme, the police, the health service and social services will therefore be particularly important. If inpatient treatment is not warranted, the probation officer may be able to identify suitable accommodation in a bail hostel or lodging scheme organised by the probation service, or by the social services. Intervention at this stage can prevent unnecessary remands to prison establishments.

CONCLUSION

25. It is the government's policy to divert mentally disordered persons from the criminal justice system in cases where the public interest does not require their prosecution. Where prosecution is necessary it is important to find suitable non-penal disposals wherever appropriate and the police, courts, and probation service are asked to work together with their local health and social services to make effective use of the provisions of the Mental Health Act 1983 and of the services which exist to help the mentally disordered. They are also asked to ensure that all their officers are aware of this circular, and to consider any training which is necessary to equip them in their contacts with mentally disordered persons.

26. In summary:

    (i) Chief officers of police are asked to ensure that, taking into account of the public interest, consideration is always given to alternatives to prosecuting mentally disordered offenders, including taking no further action where appropriate and that effective arrangements are established with local health and social services authorities to ensure their speedy involvement when mentally disordered persons are taken into police custody;

    (ii) Courts are asked to ensure that alternatives to custody are considered for all mentally disordered persons, including bail before sentence, and that persons who are in need of medical treatment are not sent to prison. The attention of court clerks is drawn, in particular, to the desirability of establishing arrangements in cooperation with the probation service and the local health and social services authorities, for speedy access to professional advice for the court to assist it in its decision making;

    (iii) Chief probation officers are asked to ensure that effective arrangements are established to provide courts with information and advice to enable them to make use of alternatives to imprisonment in dealing with mentally disordered offenders. Attention is drawn to the need to co-operate with local health and social services authorities to provide professional advice to courts and to facilitate a wider use of treatment and non-custodial disposals, including remands on bail before sentence and psychiatric probation orders and guardianship orders, where appropriate, after conviction; and

    (iv) prison medical officers are asked to ensure that action is taken to arrange transfer to hospital under the provisions of section 48 of the Mental Health Act 1983 in respect of any mentally ill or severely mentally impaired person remanded in custody who appears to require urgent treatment in hospital, and to consider advising the courts of the suitability of any other mentally disordered person on remand for treatment as part of a non-custodial disposal, such as a psychiatric probation order or guardianship order, after conviction. Prison medical officers are asked to ensure that action is taken to arrange the transfer to hospital under the provisions of section 47 of the Mental Health Act 1983 of any sentenced prisoner who appears to require treatment in hospital for mental disorder.

Mental Health Act 1983 Code of Practice: extracts from Chapter 3

Assessment by a doctor

3.7 A doctor who is asked to provide an opinion in relation to a possible admission under Part III of the Act should:

(a) identify him or herself to the person being assessed, explain who has requested the report and the limits of confidentiality in relation to the report, including that the data and the opinion could be relevant not only to medical disposal by the Court but also to the imposition of a punitive sentence, or to its length (see para 3.12);

(b) request relevant pre-sentence reports, the Inmate Medical Record, if there is one, previous psychiatric reports as well as relevant documentation regarding the alleged offence. If any of this information is not available, the doctor's report should say so clearly.

The report should, where possible, be prepared by a doctor who has previously treated the patient. The doctor, or one of them if two doctors are preparing reports, should have access to a bed or take responsibility for referring the case to another doctor who does (see para 3.18).

3.8 The doctor should, where possible, identify and access other independent sources of information about the person's previous history (including convictions), including information from GP records, previous psychiatric treatment and patterns of behaviour.

3.9 Assessment for admission of the patient is the responsibility of the doctor but other members of the clinical team who would be involved with the person's care and treatment should also be consulted. A nursing assessment should usually be undertaken if admission to hospital is likely to be recommended. The doctor should also contact the person who is preparing a pre-sentence report, especially if psychiatric treatment is recommended as a condition of a probation order.

3.10 In cases where the doctor cannot state with confidence at the time of sentencing whether admission to hospital will be beneficial, he or she should consider recommending an interim hospital order under section 38 of the Act. This order provides for the person to be admitted to hospital for up to 12 weeks (which may be extended for further periods of up to 28 days to a maximum total of 12 months) so that recommendations as to treatability and the appropriateness of continuing treatment in hospital can be fully informed.

Reports to the court

3.11 The weight of the clinical opinion is particularly important in helping courts to determine the sentence to be passed. In the case of patients subject to criminal proceedings the doctor's report should be set out clearly:

(a) the data on which the report is based;

(b) how this relates to the opinion given;

(c) where relevant, how the opinion may relate to any medical condition defence, or other trial issue;

(d) factors relating to the presence of mental disorder that may affect the risk that the patient poses to him or herself, or to others, including the risk of re-offending; and

(e) if admission to hospital is recommended, what, if any, special treatment or security is required and how this would be addressed.

The report should not comment on guilt or innocence.

3.12 When sentencing mentally disordered offenders the court is bound by the requirement in section 4 of the Criminal Justice Act 1991 to consider any information before it which relates to the patient's mental condition. Except where the offence is one for which the law requires a life sentence the court must, before passing sentence, consider the effect of a custodial sentence on the offender's mental disorder and on the treatment which may be available for it.

APPENDIX 7

Guidance from the criminal law committee of the Law Society

ADVISING A JUVENILE, MENTALLY DISORDERED OR MENTALLY HANDICAPPED SUSPECT IN THE POLICE STATION WHEN AN APPROPRIATE ADULT IS PRESENT

1. When a suspect seeks advice from a solicitor, what is said between them will be protected by the solicitor's duty to keep information confidential.

2. The codes of practice made under the Police and Criminal Evidence Act 1984 require the police to call an 'appropriate adult' to the police station if the suspect is a juvenile or a mentally disordered or mentally handicapped person.

3. Difficulties may sometimes arise when the appropriate adult is present during a consultation between a solicitor and the suspect. Such a consultation may not be subject to public interest immunity from disclosure. A social worker's role is different from that of a solicitor as they have other interests to consider besides those of the suspect. There is a risk that the appropriate adult may then disclose what was said during that consultation to the police as their code of conduct allows them to breach confidentiality in this way if they believe that the safety of the public may be at risk from the suspect.

4.1 To ensure that a suspect has the opportunity of confidential consultations with their solicitor it is recommended that the suspect is at first advised, in the appropriate adult's absence, about the risk of disclosure.

4.2 A problem may arise with a mentally disordered or mentally handicapped person who may not be able to understand the risk of disclosure. The appropriate adult may be of help to the solicitor in clarifying whether the person is able to comprehend this.

4.3 The question of whether the appropriate adult's presence is desirable or not during any further consultations between the suspect and the solicitor can then be considered in consultation with the appropriate adult, taking into account any risk of disclosure and the wishes of the client who may find reassurance in the presence of an appropriate adult whom they know.

5.1 In the next edition of the Society's guidelines for solicitors 'Advising a suspect in the police station' amendments will be made to para. 10.1.4(B) (p.47) about advising juvenile suspects. That paragraph will include the advice: 'At the police station, first advise the juvenile alone about the risk of disclosure by

113

the appropriate adult. A decision can then be made in consultation with the appropriate adult, about whether the appropriate adult should be present during any further consultations, taking into account the suspect's wishes and any risk of disclosure.'

5.2 The guidelines already state that identical considerations apply to advice to a mentally disordered or mentally handicapped person.

Gazette [1993], 19 May.

Useful addresses

Association of Police Surgeons

18A Mount Parade, Harrogate, North Yorkshire HG1 1BX

British Medical Association

BMA House Tavistock Square, London WC1
020 7387 4499

General Medical Council

178–202 Great Portland Street, London W1N 6JE
020 7580 7642

Home Office

Mental Health Unit, 50 Queen Anne's Gate, London SW1H 9AT
020 7273 4000

Law Society

Mental Health and Disability Sub-committee
The Law Society, 113 Chancery Lane, London WC2A 1PL
020 7242 1222

Legal Aid Board Head Office

85 Gray's Inn Road, London WC1X 8AA
020 7813 1000

MACA (Mental After Care Association)

25 Bedford Square, London WC1B 3HW
020 7436 6194

MENCAP (Royal Society for Mentally Handicapped Children and Adults)

National Centre, 123 Golden Lane, London EC1.
020 7454 0454

Mental Health Act Commission

Maid Marian House, 56 Hounds Gate, Nottingham NG1 6BG
0115 943 7100

Mental Health Foundation

20–21 Cornwall Terrace, London NW1 4QL
020 7535 7400

MIND (National Association for Mental Health)

Head Office, Granta House, 15–19 Broadway, London E15.
020 8519 2122

NACRO (National Association for the Care and Resettlement of Offenders)

169 Clapham Road, London SW9 OPU
020 7582 6500

National Association of Probation Officers

4 Chivalry Road, London SW11 1HT
020 7223 4887

National Schizophrenia Fellowship

28 Castle Street, Kingston-Upon-Thames, Surrey KT1 1SS
020 8547 3937

Royal College of Psychiatrists

17 Belgrave Square, London SW1
020 7235 2351

Sainsbury Centre for Mental Health

134–138 Borough High Street, London SE1 1LB
020 7403 8790

SANE (Schizophrenia – A National Emergency)

1st Floor, Cityside House, 40 Adler Street, London E1 1EE
020 7375 1002; Helpline 0345 678000

Voice UK

The College Business Centre, Uttoxeter New Road, Derby DE22 3WZ
01332 202555

Zito Trust

PO Box 265, London WC2
020 7240 8422

Bibliography

Ashford, M. and Chard, A. *Defending Young People in the Criminal Justice System*, 2nd edn (Legal Action Group, 2000).

Association of Police Surgeons *The Role of the Independent Forensic Physician* (August 1996).

Association of Police Surgeons *The Safety and Security of the Administration of Medication in Police Custody: Guidelines for Forensic Physicians and Custodians* (February 1997).

Best Practice Advisory Group *Mentally Disordered Offenders* (Lord Chancellor's Department, July 1992).

Bull and Cullen *Witnesses who have Mental Handicaps* (The Crown Office, Edinburgh, 1992).

Cape, E. with Luqmani, J. *Defending Suspects at Police Stations: The Practitioner's Guide to Advice and Representation* (Legal Action Group, 1999).

Clare, I. and Gudjonsson, G. *et al.* 'The vulnerability of suspects with intellectual disabilities during police interviews: a review and experimental study of decision-making', British Journal of Learning Disabilities, 8:2 (1995), 110-28.

Ede, R. and Shepherd, E. *Active Defence: A Lawyer's Guide to Police and Defence Investigation and Prosecution and Defence Disclosure in Criminal Cases*, revised 1st edn (The Law Society, 1998).

Edwards, A. *Advising a Suspect at the Police Station*, 4th edn (Sweet & Maxwell, 1997).

Eldergill, A. *Mental Health Review Tribunals: Law and Practice* (Sweet & Maxwell, 1997).

General Medical Council *Confidentiality: Guidance to Doctors* (October 1995).

General Medical Council *Seeking Patients' Consent: the Ethical Considerations* (February 1999).

Hallmark, R. MIND *Psychiatric Legal Dictionary* (MIND, 1997).

Heaton-Armstrong, A., Shepherd, E. and Wolchover, D. *Analysing Witness Testimony*, (Blackstone Press, 1999).

Hodgson, J. 'Vulnerable suspects and the appropriate adult', *Criminal Law Review* (November 1997).

Hollins, Murphy and Claire *You're on Trial*, Books Beyond Words (Gashell Press/St George's Hospital Medical School, London 1996).

Home Office Circular 66/1990 'Provision for Mentally Disordered' (September 1990).

Home Office Circular 22/1992 'Principles of Investigative Interviewing' (1992).

Home Office Circular 29/1993 'Community Care reforms and the Criminal Justice System' (1993).

Home Office Circular 18/1994 'Cautioning' (1994).

Home Office Circular 12/1995 'Mentally Disordered Offenders: Inter-Agency Working' (May 1995).

Home Office Circular 52/1997 'Crime (Sentences) Act 1997' (October 1997).
Jones, R. *Mental Health Act Manual* 6th edn (Sweet & Maxwell, 1999).
Laing, J. 'The mentally disordered suspect at the police station', *Criminal Law Review* (1995).
Law Society *Guide to the Professional Conduct of Solicitors 1999*, 8th edn (Law Society Publishing, 1999).
Law Society *Mental Health and Disability Sub Committee Guidelines for Legal Representatives at Mental Health Tribunals* (May 1998).
Legal Aid Board *Legal Aid Handbook 1998-9* (Sweet & Maxwell, 1999).
Littlechild, B. *The Police and Criminal Evidence Act 1984: The Role of the Appropriate Adult* (BASW Trading, 1996).
Prins, H. 'Risk assessment and management in criminal justice and psychiatry' *Journal of Forensic Psychiatry* 7:1 (May 1996).
Report of the Independent Inquiry into the care and treatment of Adrian Jones and Douglas Heathwaite, commissioned by County Durham Health Authority (August 1998).
Report of the Inquiry into the Care and Treatment of Christopher Edwards and Richard Linford, commissioned by North Essex Health Authority, Essex County Council and HM Prison Service. (1998).
Royal Commission on Criminal Justice *The Role of the Police Surgeons*, Research Study No. 6 (HMSO, 1992).
Shepherd, E. *Police Station Skills for Legal Advisers* 2nd edn, (4 vols with 2 cassettes) (The Law Society, 1994).
Voice UK, *Competent to Tell the Truth* (Voice UK 1998)
Ward, T. 'Magistrates, insanity and the common law', *Criminal Law Review* (November 1997).

Index